Church Unity

and

Church Mission

Church Unity
and
Church Mission

by

MARTIN E. MARTY

WM. B. EERDMANS PUBLISHING COMPANY
GRAND RAPIDS, MICH. / LONDON

PHOTOLITHOPRINTED BY GRAND RAPIDS BOOK MANUFACTURERS, INC.
GRAND RAPIDS, MICHIGAN

To Past and Present Editors of
THE CHRISTIAN CENTURY
Sympathetic Critics and
Critical Sympathists of
the Ecumenical Movement

PREFACE

HAD THIS BOOK A SUBTITLE IT COULD BE: "A RADICAL AP-
proach for Conservative Christians." By "radical" I would not
mean "left-wing" but "going to the root," and by "conservative" not "right-wing" but "holding to the tradition." *Church
Unity and Church Mission* tries never to lose sight of the fact
that many people who want to be faithful to the Church's received doctrine are impatient with the ecumenical movement. So far as I know, no book is at present directed to
include these among its audience, along with those others who
have been accustomed to being favorable to ecumenical
strivings or who have remained content with its achievements.

The author is in no way connected with any of the official ecumenical organizations, though he is related to a
journal which has sought to relate itself to the variety of
movements to Christian unity, and to an interdenominational
institution of Christian higher education. He has no reasons
for making an apology for the ecumenical institutions and
this book does not do so. This does not mean that the
author has no admiration for the inspirers and agents of
ecumenical organization. It does mean that he carries no
burden of administration and is in no sense dependent upon
its destiny for his personal security.

Why was the book written?

First, because a publisher asked for it. 1960 was an
"ecumenical summer." The Faith and Order Commission,
the World Student Christian Commission, the Eucharistic
Congress, the World Council of Churches' Central Committee

and the ecumenically-oriented youth of Europe — among others — held meetings. I had poked my journalist's nose in on many of these and had summarized impressions in shorthand form in a series of magazine articles. An intended book on the subject never moved beyond first draft, however, because Pope John XXIII threw the ecumenical movement into an entirely different setting by his establishment of a Secretariat to promote Christian unity and by his call for a Council.

The year 1963 provided many new opportunities for an appraisal. The Faith and Order Conference met; some world confessional bodies (Anglican and Lutheran in particular) met; a new pope was preparing a second conclave of the Vatican Council; the 1961 meeting of the World Council of Churches at New Delhi was far enough into the past that its legacy could be dealt with. As I prepared to report on some of these events the publisher asked that I finally prepare the manuscript to incorporate them. Every line of the earlier draft had to be rewritten in the light of changed situations. It would not have been written at all had he not encouraged its development in a field in which change is constant.

For the rest, it is almost easier to say what the reasons for writing were *not*. I am in no way awed by the workings of ecumenical organizations and would hardly think of viewing an ecumenical gatherings' robed procession as an exciting way to spend an afternoon. Nor am I motivated by a passion for the concept of "unity" in the abstract sense or for mere "oneness" to tidy up a world of bewildering variety. The pages which follow will reveal the extent to which one need not cope with abstract ideas about "essential unity" nor prefer "one" to "many" on general principles. As a matter of fact, the pages which follow will provide numbers of opportunities to contend for variety, diversity, texture, color, regionalism, inherited heterogeneity, wonder, and surprise.

What is left is the one concern made clear in the title: a

missionary sense which decries all competition and implied undercutting of others' witness to one Lord. This may be a brutally functional way of looking at "the doctrine of unity." Most of my time is spent, however, with people whose first consciousness is not one of the Church looking at itself, but rather one of the world looking at itself without allowing much elbowroom for the Church or the Christian claim. Few in the latter are going to become involved with the cause of Jesus Christ because of revisions in jurisdictions of the Church or negotiations between churchly committees, however important these may be. Sometimes, however, they may be open to a view of the Church that acts in such a way that its embarrassment to the world's ways and its proposals for the world's future cannot be neglected. They may also listen to people thinking, talking, and theologizing about the Church in the world.

Unfortunately, the disciplines of life are growing so technical and are becoming so separated that the language of one does not mean much to intelligent people who are caught up with another. My attempt to combine churchly interests and their overlays of language with some of the speech used by people "on the outside" may be unsuccessful, but someone must continue these experiments until someone else succeeds with them.

This manuscript was completed as the last act of a career outside the academy and the assumptions of the academic community. Soon, instead of writing missionary tracts, I may be called to prepare more formal histories of the Church in our day, in which the ecumenical movement plays so large a part. If so, this personal document can stand as a serious tract, a well-meant argument by a "missionary" to whom the cause of Christian unity stands in the highest incidental relation.

I thank *The Christian Century* for subsidizing and encouraging my ecumenical summers and the many leaders of the movement for permitting interviews and for releasing many ideas which have had to be plagiarized without acknowledgment on these pages.

— MARTIN E. MARTY

The University of Chicago

The Commemoration of St. Augustine, August 28, 1963

CONTENTS

Preface   7

Introduction: Too Fast and Too Slow   13

1. "Why Don't the Churches Get Together?"   23

2. The Confusion of Directives.
   Love Thy Neighbor; Shove Thy Neighbor   38

3. "The Ecumenical Movement Hasn't Caught On"   48

4. The Unity Which Divides Us   61

5. Unity: Everywhere But Nowhere   76

6. A Complication Which Simplifies   100

7. The Death and Birth of Discipline or:
   Every Man Has His Own Ecumenical Movement   118

8. Back to the Wall; Face to the World   129

11

Of God: *God does not command impossible things. But, as he commands, he asks us to do what we can — and also to ask for what we cannot.*

Of others: *Whether they like it or not, they are our brothers. They will only cease to be our brothers when they cease to say, "Our Father."*

Odisse errores, diligere errantes.
— ST. AUGUSTINE

INTRODUCTION:
TOO FAST AND TOO SLOW

IN THE PAST, WHEN WRITERS WANTED PEOPLE IN THE churches to hear, they would write what they called tracts for their times. They would speak in the simpler language of the Church, to make themselves clear. Today men do not often speak or hear that language. Even the simpler words of Christian usage have to be explained. Sometimes they are too familiar to carry fresh ideas. More often they are too unfamiliar. An author who wants to hold the hearing of intelligent people who do not happen to make their living "talking Christian words" does well to avoid the private words which Christian thinkers employ.

If this little book had been written three years earlier we would have had a problem of language with its chief word. We will talk very much about the word *ecumenical*, which is concerned with the movement or spirit which seeks to find and to show forth the oneness of Jesus Christ's Church in the whole world. Now we do not have to explain too much. Perhaps, for this happy change, we should send a card of thanks to the late Pope John XXIII. For fifty years the ecumenical movement had been thriving, but the man of the workaday world was little aware of it. If he ever heard the word which gave the movement its name he would be puzzled. Public curiosity grew, however, when newspaper headlines began to report on Pope John's call for an ecumenical council. Today we can use this private and technical word of the churches in many ways without having to explain.

This book will often concern itself with the ecumenical *movement*. By that we mean to refer to the few great and many smaller world-wide attempts to form organizations which will watch the day-to-day life of the uniting spirit. More often, however, it will deal with the ecumenical *spirit*. This will refer to the attitudes and motives among Christian people which produce actions and realities evident to the world. The distinction is important and has to do with the main theme of the book.

At the moment our understanding of the ecumenical spirit is hampered by the modern world's fascination with organizations and clubs and institutions. Whoever happens to belong to a Christian group or club or denomination which happens to belong to "the ecumenical movement" is considered somehow automatically to have the ecumenical spirit as well. Actually, he may be unaware of this belonging. Or he may use it to justify himself before God. He may even be in such an organization while actually opposing its purposes. Meanwhile, whoever happens not to have an organizational link with the movement is considered somehow automatically to be non- or anti-ecumenical. He may even believe so himself.

None of this talk about whether one is ecumenical in spirit or not should make any difference if all that were being bantered about is a person's status in the public sphere of Christianity. Surely, toward the end of the twentieth century it is considered "the thing to do" to belong to an ecumenically-directed church! Something more important than proper affiliations and badges is at stake. When we discuss the ecumenical spirit we deal with the central reality and central purpose of the Church of Jesus Christ. As such it has to do with a question of truth itself. If the Church is really one, then he who finds no way of asserting his faith in this reality and no way of expressing it is a denier of the truth. Pity him if he excludes himself because he does not belong to the right club! Pity him more if he does belong and if that fact is meaningless to him.

Let me speak for a moment in words which seem at first to contradict each other. If we survey a half-century and especially the most recent half-decade of striving, we can say: the ecumenical movement is proceeding *too rapidly* for Christians to grasp and keep up with its forms. Advances undreamed of three or four years ago are considered commonplace now; but they are hardly assimilated by the Church at large. Yet, on the other hand, each advance is still filled with so many problems that we can now turn the phrase around and speak of *tardiness*. The Christian who wants to think and work in the world as a Christian dare not wait for the ecumenical intention to reach its stated goals and become a fulfilled reality. The ecumenical movement is far too slow, too undramatic, too frustrating for that.

The argument of this book will center on the idea that we now *have* enough unity for the Church to resume its mission to the world and to do this in a new way. To complete the circle: if Christians resume their mission and do this mindful of the newness involved, they will find more unity in Christ and will learn more motives for seeking it. If, on the other hand, they sit back with report card in hand awaiting the final outcome of the ecumenical movement, they can easily paralyze the movement itself.

Christians assert that no unity exists in the Church other than that which God provides. In this sense, a half-century ago there was a hidden unity which was obscured by men's visible disunity as Christians; but it is hard to speak precisely about this unity. Similarly, we dare not be so brash as to speak of the hidden disunity which masquerades behind the visible unity of Christians in their organizations today. But what is visible helps or hinders the Church's thought and work. If that is true, we can rightfully contrast the world of 1910 with that of today.

Think, then, of 1910. For almost one thousand years the Christians of Western Europe and the Western world were largely cut off from those of the East. Usually there was lack of interest or ignorance to separate them. Sometimes there had been hostility and open warfare. Only very rarely and momentarily had men of good will from either side shown interest in approaching the other. For the better part of half those thousand years Christians of the West had been divided after the Reformation. The same kind of alternating hot and cold wars — strange words to use of Christians! — had prevailed. Within the Protestant minority in the West there had been nothing but division and separation and attempts to justify these divisions through hostility to other Christians in the name of the truth which was being denied through hostility.

Today, in the formal sense, the intentions of most Christians of the world and their leaders have been changed. Today most Protestant Christians belong to churches which themselves belong to the ecumenical movement. Thus, no matter how lukewarm and halfhearted they are as Christians, they are considered to be "ecumenical" and formally they are involved in showing forth the unity of Christ's Church. Today the Roman Catholic Church is very busy expressing its own inner concerns for unity throughout the world. What is more, in surprising varieties of ways since 1959, this church has concerned itself with Orthodox and Protestant Christians. It has established means of staying in contact with the Orthodox-Protestant ecumenical movement. In 1963, at an important meeting of the movement at Montreal, Father Gregory Baum publicly expressed himself in dramatic form: the Roman Catholic Church had no doctrinal reason — only practical and pastoral ones — for not being in the Orthodox-Protestant movement's chief cluster of emphases called the World Council of Churches and its Faith and Order element, which concerns itself with Christian truth and theology. And what of Orthodoxy? This large minority of Christians, so mysterious in the eyes of most Roman and Protestant Christians, no longer is hidden from their view. However much its doctrine of the Church forces it to look on other churches as a sort of shadow or partial church, Orthodoxy is now a full and energetic participant in the ecumenical movement. This is true also across the lines of man-made political barriers such as the Iron Curtain. A fourth and smaller (by far) cluster of churches has not to this date formally joined the ecumenical movement. (A tiny minority in this cluster, as a matter of fact, has joined in anti-ecumenical movements!) This book will concern itself as much with members of these latter churches as it will with the problems of halfheartedness among members of others.

What shall we call these churches in the Christian world's fourth family? There is as much variety here as among the denominations which make up ecumenically-formed Protestant-ism or among the regions of Orthodoxy or the many ex-pressions of Roman Catholicism. I suppose no attempt at naming will be so satisfying and clarifying or so inclusive as the distinction used by William Richey Hogg in his fine brief book *One World, One Mission* (New York: Friendship, 1960, pp. 68ff.). In an all-business manner and without the slightest attempt to be clever or memorable Hogg lists four categories of Christians:

1. *Roman Catholics*
2. *Eastern Orthodox*
3. *Protestants Within the Ecumenical Movement*
4. *Protestants Not in the Ecumenical Movement.*

He also includes a footnote about the fact that he cannot deal with Unitarians, Christian Scientists, Mormons, etc.

The last two categories interest us. They are forthrightly stated. Alas! the phrases are too long and cumbersome for regular use in this book and we shall have to adopt some shorthand. More and more people in the fourth cluster are coming to call themselves "the evangelicals." In many ways we can be uneasy with the term. There are too many evangelicals in Orthodox, Roman, and ecumenically Protestant Christianity who seem to be excluded. Similarly, there are too many ecumenically-involved people in "evangelicalism" to see this factor in their lives dismissed. What is more, in many parts of the world to apply the term "evangelical" to groups outside the ecumenical movement would be meaningless or foolish. If we want seriously to play the game of who owns which shorthand word we should recognize that *all* informed Christians make some sort of claim to be ecumenical ("one"), catholic ("catholic"), and orthodox or evangelical ("apostolic") in that Church whose fourth mark is "holy."

We are, however, writing in the context of North America, and we are trying to pay some attention to what people call themselves. "Evangelical" means oriented toward the good news of God's action in Jesus Christ. We shall often let it stand in this book to describe "Protestants Not in the Ecumenical Movement" whether they are actually evangelical or ecumenical or not. The setting of the word will help the reader learn which use is implied.[1]

While this book and its argument will no doubt have little effect on the belligerently anti-ecumenical evangelical partisans — though we might hope that it may — it will constantly keep in mind that vast majority of "Protestants Not in the Ecumenical Movement" who have shown some kind of interest in the ecumenical spirit.

This brief reference to the game of labels and names serves to introduce issues represented inside and around the

---

[1] *Ecumenism and the Evangelical* by J. Marcellus Kik (Philadelphia: Presbyterian and Reformed Publishing Company, 1958) is an example — unfortunately a rather belligerent one — of the custom of taking "evangelical" as an alternative to "ecumenical" for granted in speech.

ecumenical movement. To the ecumenically-oriented, "evangelicalism" is interested in its version of truth at the expense of Christian unity. To the evangelical, the ecumenical Christian is interested in his version of unity at the expense of Christian truth. The poles of unity (which has to overcome centuries of differing expressions of Christian truth) and truth (which is obscured by the disunited expressions) remain at the heart of ecumenical talk. They have helped bring the conversation to its current stale point. Misunderstanding of both will, according to the argument of these chapters, serve to preoccupy the churches, distract them from mission and work, and in the end defeat the interests of both truth and unity.

Supposedly, the people who have opposed the ecumenical movement from within or without in the name of Christian truth have done so for a clear reason. They believe that to converse or work with Christians who see many matters far differently than themselves will serve to compromise their own truth. Such action will lead people to think that doctrine is unimportant, to become indifferent to the claims of truth. By standing apart and being "particular" over against other Christians they feel they will better serve as custodians and teachers of Christian truth. If we take the whole picture into view, however, we must say that things have not worked out that way. In fact, this strategy has worked against itself; it has caused the world to dismiss the quest for Christian truth and caused Christians to become indifferent to the claim of truth because of the varieties of competing claims. Numbers of studies of the actual beliefs and the actual knowledge of Christian people make this clear. Ecumenical interest in theology and Christian thought, on the other hand, however weak it has been, has made the quest for truth a public matter, familiar even in the newspaper headlines.

Evangelicalism has thus worked against its own purpose and many of its leaders are reappraising past strategies. Intense if often prejudiced interest is shown in intra-Christian conversation about the things of God. Many "Protestants Not in the Ecumenical Movement" have become better informed than those in it. At every ecumenical gathering large numbers of non-member observers participate with passion and often with learning and sympathy. They have recognized the extent and depth of the ecumenical spirit which now sets the terms for theology. Today most serious Christian thought is directed to the concerns of the whole Church and not just to a particular portion of it.

If this is so and if this understanding spreads, the day may come when evangelicals may learn that they can better serve their own purposes within the ecumenical movement. In that instance they will simply take on a different teaching task. Whereas in the past they have suggested that only aloofness indicates seriousness (and here they have failed to teach effectively), now they would have to indicate that acceptance of others in ecumenical word and work does not imply indifferentism to the quest for truth. Since such a step would be taken consciously and would summon fresh energies, we may have some confidence that such churches would have more success with this approach than they did when they were aloof.

By now it should be clear that this book is written around one simple theme. It has no interest in producing new light on the documents of the ecumenical movement. It wants instead to provoke Christian people into thinking about one theme: that they have enough unity now to resume their mission to the world, and that resumed mission will enhance the quest for unity. The link between the two is a kind of imagination not often shown either by the halfhearted ecumenical or by the uninterested evangelical Christian.

The imagination which links unity and mission was revealed for the first time and the best time in that prayer which has motivated so much of the ecumenical spirit. In the familiar prayer of Jesus as reproduced in John 17:20ff.: "I do not pray for these only, but also for those who are to believe in me through their word, that they may all be one; even as thou, Father, art in me, and I in thee, that they also may be in us, *so that* the world may believe that thou hast sent me." Again in verses 22-23 the text records a prayer "that they may be one even as we [the Father and Jesus] are one . . . *so that* the world may know. . . ." I am aware that there are many interpretations and misinterpretations of John 17; there are many misuses of the text and many ways of using it to avoid what it says. Interpreting the passage as a whole is extremely difficult. Here we are interested only in two simple and obvious words: "so that." Whatever else happens under the category of unity between Father and Jesus and between disciple and disciple, and whatever happens when disciple meets world, the two "whatevers" are connected by a "so that." Each exists for the other and the one does not happen without the other — otherwise, why pray for this to happen?

So long as the "so that" phrase is above the doorpost of every ecumenical meeting and so long as it burns in the heart and gives guidance to the eye, the reuniting movement can keep its sense of purpose. Without that phrase the movement is constantly in danger of becoming a hobby for the few.

Judged from the viewpoint of the work which should be enhanced by Christian unity, the efforts of the past half-century have been impressive. Since, however, the work or the mission constantly slips from view, the movement is daily threatened and on the verge of stalemate. After most ecumenical gatherings of recent years — one thinks particularly of the meetings of the Faith and Order emphasis of the World Council of Churches at Lund, Sweden (1952) and Montreal, Canada (1963) — there are widespread complaints by participants that a new plateau has been reached, that future direction is unclear. Such a complaint provides the opportunity to ask the questions of original purpose and final goal. Such times are the moments for the exercise of Christian imagination.

So long as all goes according to plan and elements of the ecumenical movement fit together neatly, little imagination is necessary. When new elements are introduced: the Russian churches join; the Pope calls a council; then, when the Protestant churches are uncertain, Christians can afford to be more radical. "For the form of this world is passing away" (I Cor. 7:31); this reality is recognized most clearly when the Church is most uncertain.

In this moment, when the ecumenical intention has become so clear so rapidly that we cannot grasp it, and when the ecumenical reality is coming about so slowly that men risk being bored, it is time to ask what is the purpose of the movement toward unity. There seems to be no way to do this without examining the ecumenical movement against the background of what the world and the Church expect.

Chapter One

"WHY DON'T THE CHURCHES
GET TOGETHER?"

A PROFESSLONAL HISTORY OF THE TWENTIETH-CENTURY ECU-
menical movement will not serve us well if we wish to see
this movement in the light of the world's question. As a formal
force the movement does not hold interest long. It soon
is seen to be a matter of churchly housekeeping and placing
of furniture. There is no particular reason why an African
anti-colonial or an American anti-clerical should bother himself with the detail of such housekeeping. He will take notice
only of "the main point" expressed in his familiar question
— if he has any glimmer of interest — "Why don't the
churches get together?"

The way the question is put is very revealing. The
questioner is also captive of the mentality of the era of complex organizations. He does not ask, "Why don't Christian
people get together?" or, "Why does not Christian unity show
itself?" He sees great blocs of Christians called Catholic and
Orthodox, Methodist and Presbyterian at war with each other
or quietly disputing each other's claims. He can foresee no
advance of unity until these blocs come to understanding or
join forces. He should not be blamed for putting the question
in this way; this is how most Christian people also see the
issue. As soon as he hears, "They are trying," he is a bit
reassured about the attempt, a bit disdainful of the difficulties,
and totally bored over details.

23

Actually, despite the modern form that his organizational question takes, there is a profound Christian instinct behind it. Among the New Testament's many images of the Church none is so rich or vivid as that which compares it to a living body of which Christ is the living head. The first reality of a living Church should be that it suggests a living tie between the two. Instead, there is an apparent gap which many churches claim to bridge. This is the fatal interval which defeats an understanding of the nature of the Church and limits a view of its real work. "For between the Body and the Head there is no room for any interval — if there were any, there would be neither Head nor Body" (St. John Chrysostom). To the rejecting modern there is no Head — only a dead Christ who belongs to history — and there is no Body; there are only corpses.

Ask a devoted Christian, "Why might *you* ask, 'Why don't the churches get together?' ?" He might answer, "I do not have to ask; I know they are trying." Or he might say, "Because I know it is the nature of the Church to be one"; or, "Because I find Christian competition distasteful." But for him such a qutstion would be one among many in church life. He remains a faithful participant in the affairs and concerns of a local congregation and perhaps a denomination. From time to time he may take notice of ecumenical affairs, but frustration over them does not deter him from Christian action on other fronts. The man outside the Church asks the question because, whether from good motives or bad, from understanding or misunderstanding, he sees that it obscures the basic nature of the Church. Until some satisfactory answer is given him, he can cancel divided Christianity out of the daily concerns of his life.

Today's Christians must be careful not to lay too much blame at their fathers' doors; let each historical period take care of its own repentance. Thus if we ask why this question did not deter Christian missions in that century when they are regarded to have been so successful (the nineteenth), we cannot answer it in terms of the twentieth century. In the past century churches still knew the geographical luxury of enjoying separation. In the back of people's minds Christian division might have been offensive and Christian missionary competition distasteful. But the man who lived in the Orthodox East or in a Catholic nation or region of the West did not experience division as a day-to-day reality. A Methodist in a Methodist town in Iowa was not likely to be offended by the reality that Swedish Lutherans had a church separated from his own in a rural valley some miles away. Changes in modern life, particularly the "image-consciousness" created by mass media and human interaction based on new kinds of mobility, have made people aware of competing kinds of Christianity.

When was the problem of competing claims as a complication of mission first perceived? Read the writings of the real pioneers of nineteenth-century Christian missionary or benevolent work and you will find on almost every page an increasing sense of anguish over separation.

Admittedly this anguish was not always informed by a desire to do something about the problem or a knowledge of how to do it. Ordinarily it was assumed that the problem would be solved if only everyone else would come around to "my" point of view. Seldom was there real examination of the accidents which went into making up "my" point of view. But as the nineteenth century drew to a close (many historians date its end in 1914 with the beginning of the great war), forward-looking people from the mission field began to seek means of commending Christ to the world through a united Church. The concern led to the missionary meeting in Scotland (Edinburgh, 1910) from which the Protestant and now the inclusive ecumenical movement of modern times can date itself. The questions of students, the concerns of laymen, the anguish of missionaries — these led to the beginnings of the reunitive effort. This is the fundamental fact of ecumenicity, that it was based on questions relating to mission and service. Each refreshment of ecumenical concern from Edinburgh through the Vatican Council has meant an attempt to recover the questions imposed by laymen, students, and missionaries. Every departure from the original question, every bogging down of the ecumenical spirit into a tiring institutionalism, has come from failure to recall the basic question.

Such is the nature of institutions that they may take on a self-propagating life independent of original purpose. "The same institutions that men create in their common thought and action become an independent power and impose their own laws upon the very hearts of these men."[1] Nowhere was this reality made more clear than when, in 1960-61, the International Missionary Council (the most inclusive missionary organization) was integrated into the World Council of Churches (the most inclusive ecumenical organization). The entire matter was a bureaucratic shift. It did not become a part of the daily consciousness of Christian students, laymen, and missionaries — if indeed they heard about it at all!

To laud students, laymen, and missionaries is not the same thing as to romanticize them. Without doubt these instigators of ecumenicity were from the human point of view naive in their biblical exegesis. They may have oversimplified questions of Christian theology which professional academicians must pursue. They have been neglectful of many kinds of pastoral concerns which could still be carried on in separated Christianity. But the vision of an emerging world belonged to them.

Now fifty years later the impatient question of the most concerned church people has passed to the lips of the most indifferent ones, and particularly to those who are not of

[1] A. Gehlen, *Urmensch und Spätkultur* (Bonn: Athenaeum Verlag, 1956), p. 9.

the churches at all. "Why don't the churches get together?" At numbers of ecumenical meetings my purpose in a city will be questioned by a taxicab driver. (These drivers have taken over the religious role which the Delphic oracle once possessed.) As soon as I say I am attending a meeting which seeks to foster religious harmony, all is well. Soon we are back to discussing baseball or hockey or rugby (ecumenical gatherings and cab drivers are world-wide phenomena), but not before he has passed judgment on the meeting: "That's good." Whether religious or nonreligious, whether out of impatience with confusion or from being sick and tired of all forms of human conflict, his judgment will be passed in the name of a world which pays attention to a uniting Church but which does not regard with favor or interest any version of Christianity which keeps to itself.

Something has to happen, however, if these small stirrings of interest are to be sustained. An audience in a darkened theater will wait for the curtain to rise only for a short period. Then it will applaud, not because it likes the show but because it wants the show to begin. It will be satisfied only if the show "moves," has a plot, a sense of progress, an outcome. On these pages we shall be contending that the "outcome" of the ecumenical movement which will stir the world is not an organizationally-fulfilled, undergirding and overarching Christian unity. What will be satisfying is the honest portrayal to the world of reuniting Christian churches which do not compete but do accept and support each other and which — this is most important of all — carry on together their mission of serving and saving through word and work in the world. Unless this reality is immediately and constantly telegraphed to the world, with facts to back up the assertions, the semi-interested people will resume their own talk, understandably unmindful of the churches.

To the dedicated professional of ecumenical relations there

must be something profoundly frustrating about this kind of talk. Often he dismisses it as being beside the point. Or it sounds to him as if one wants to "start from scratch" every day — and he wishes to make progress. Or he is unwilling to grant such great Christian insight to the taxicab driver and the man of the avenue or factory, whose opinions do not count for very much in other assessments of Christian work. More often, he forgets the question because it has honestly been gathered up into his own concerns; he really believes he is answering the question and in his own way he is doing just that. But he never quite understands why, despite the obviously excellent press he has received, his efforts have not been satisfying, have not caught the imagination of the world.

The ecumenical movement is, according to the most familiar phrase extended it, "the great new fact of the era." The era is, as often noted, "the century of the Church." If the biggest feature of the era's great reality is obscured, what does get through to people? Why is the ecumenical movement given only perfunctory attention by most denominational leaders themselves? Why is it notoriously the last item of a church's budget to be added and the first to disappear? Why don't books on the ecumenical movement sell? Where are the hymns of this movement comparable to the stirring, romantic songs of the preceding missionary era? These are puzzles to the man who concentrates earnestly on churchly housekeeping, institutional detail, or the theological huddle.

At the root of the problem may well be the fact that most people today are not, in any formal sense, theologically curious. Many do not ask the profound questions of life in a religious way and many who are religious do not ask them in a theological way. Perhaps part of the problem resides in what the ecumenical movement theologizes about. It has developed a private vocabulary, based on modern adaptations of the language of the New Testament, of the creed-making period, and particularly of the episode of the sixteenth-century

Protestant Reformation and Catholic counter-Reformation.

What is true of preaching, which tends to be responsive to the language interests of a definable local body of people, is more true of ecumenical theologizing. Hear Gerhard Ebeling on the problem as it relates to preaching:

> Christians have become accustomed to existence in two spheres, the sphere of the church and the sphere of the world. We have become accustomed to the co-existence of two languages, Christian language with the venerable patina of two thousand years, and the language of real life round about us. . . . Today [the problem] is acute to an unprecedented degree. For about three hundred years our world has been involved in a revolution of unheard-of extent. What we are going through today is only a phase of a revolution which goes much further back, though undoubtedly a specially stirring phase, which can make even the sleepiest of us aware of what has been going on long before our own time. For even if we are catching up only very slowly in our consciousness, whether we want to be or not we are all people of this changed world, living in it, marked by it, and responsible for it. The language of Christian preaching, on the other hand, and the way in which Christian faith is understood and expressed, spring from the period preceding that great revolution. This is not an argument against Christian faith; but it presents a task of interpretation the magnitude of which is certainly glimpsed, but of which only the first beginnings have been tackled. We must be clear that there can be no understanding of the Christian faith unless this task is undertaken.[2]

Sometimes ecumenical theologians are accused of adopting obscure churchly language as a matter of malicious choice. But why attribute to bad motives what is more likely attributable to the limits of good ones? The theologians are burdened acutely with the problem of language, while the preacher feels it temporarily and mildly. The answer will no doubt have to do with the issue: What shall the church theologize *about*

[2] Gerhard Ebeling, *The Nature of Faith*, tr. Ronald Gregor Smith (Philadelphia: Muhlenberg Press, 1961), pp. 16-17.

today? We can contend that when the works of God are seen in the works of Christ's Church as it engages in mission, in service, and in ethical decision, then the "outsider" will become curious and the theological discussion based on the churches' traditions can advance.

At a recent ecumenical gathering devoted almost wholly to theologizing (Montreal Fourth World Conference on Faith and Order, 1963) I visited the bulletin board where the press's published stories are tacked. By far the largest attention was being paid to the subject of public curiosity: the presence of delegates from behind the Iron Curtain, particularly Russia. Secondary interest was paid to the participation of the Roman Catholic Cardinal. Then followed a number of external, technical matters: How do the translators work? What about the one woman delegate? What do delegates do in their leisure time? The business of the conference, talking theology, was hardly reported on or reportable at all. Just as one may vigorously argue that churches do not need to direct all their concerns to eavesdroppers, so just as vigorously may one argue that they will make their point as churches to the degree that their thought and talk concern the real world.

No topic awakens worldly curiosity more or challenges lackadaisical Christians more than the one of Christian *mission,* if by that we mean: How does the Church commend Christ to the world through its saving words and serving works? The twentieth century poses this question differently than did the nineteenth. Then, people could assume that the Western hemisphere and Western Europe were pretty much "safe territory" from which Christians could establish beachheads in Asia, Africa, Australia, and the islands of the Pacific. Now the secularized soil of Western Europe and the strangely religious but somehow less-than-Christian environment of the Americas forces Christians to regard these as missionary fields. Then, people could choose to be active in the churches of their region or not. Now, they are allowed to pass down a whole cafeteria line of religious options and to pass up the whole menu.

If Christians are caught between two spheres of Church and world, they are also caught between public expectation and private reality, between the world of mass media's images and local realities. The world is coming to think in "metropolitan" terms while Christians are studiedly accommodated to "village" thinking. Even the most casual worlding or Christian in the worldly sphere learns to grasp realities associated with the total spiritual striving of great numbers of people. The churchman is oriented toward the competitive ministries of people in the here and now.

"Why is the quality of village interpersonal relations often so poor?" asks one student of traditional cultures. The answer: the "productive pie," the fruitful soil and its products, is limited.

> In each village tradition has determined approximately what a family may expect as its share of this small productive pie. It can expect no more, and it zealously watches to make sure it receives no less. The consequences of this situation are apparent: *if someone is seen to get ahead, logically it can only be at the expense of others in the village.* The traditional division of the pie is being upset, and the rights of all are potentially threatened.[3]

Whoever does not see in this competitive "village" concept the basic interrelation of the divided churches of Christianity has not learned to see them as the public sees them. And so long as Christians fail to gain this vision of themselves, the Christian mission cannot really be resumed. The Christian of one denomination may *read* of the work of others, but only with the lack of involvement felt by a non-investor as he looks at the stock-market news out of casual curiosity, or

[3] George M. Foster, *Traditional Cultures: and the Impact of Technological Change* (New York: Harper, 1962), pp. 52-53.

by a non-athlete looking at the batting averages without a sense that he is in the game.

Thirty-five years ago Walter Lippmann was contending that Christian teachings no longer satisfied human desires. He may be right in this claim; we cannot argue it here. But *if* spiritual hungers are being revealed today, and if to some degree these are being directed in yearning toward Christianity, we can safely note that most of these are turned toward a hope for unity in Christ. Christians believe that they have a treasure to satisfy these hopes; it is ironical that this most dramatic jewel is the one most obscured from view. It could be true that people will not again turn to Christianity on a large scale, as they did in its youth as a movement. Still, when Christianity is dismissed as dead it so often comes to life again in unexpected ways. Certainly the basic fact of Church-world relations in the twentieth century reveals an unexpected curiosity concerning the Christian vision of human solidarity. Ours is the century, says historian Arnold Toynbee, when for the first time men could conceive of doing something about the problems of the whole world (satisfying its physical hunger, etc.). In the past even this conception did not appear. So ours is the century in which nineteenth-century "beachhead" missions could be transformed into a real vision of Christ suffering and being glorified wherever men are; only in such a century will an ecumenical striving take on profound forms.

The public expectation takes many guises. "Why don't the churches get together?" could hardly be interpreted as an interest in the formation of one suffocating and all-embracing power movement. The question too often comes from the mouths of fiercely independent people. What they seek is a cessation of the competitive principle in the *practice* of Christians, so that the faith may take the form of the works which should issue from it.

In this setting what we have called "denominational particularism" has worked against itself; the non-ecumenical or anti-ecumenical who says that he wants to purify and retain truth actually barters away its seriousness. It is well known that most spokesmen for such forces or representatives of standoffish denominations have an ecumenical plan. It is very simple: join us. We are really interested in the unity of Christ's Church. But since we have an absolute and exclusive hold on the truth, we can participate only on the basis of complete capitulation and unconditional surrender by all those not lucky enough to have been born into our club. We are really working for unity by witnessing to our truth. Actually, people who talk this way can go through years of life in their churches without making a single penitent move or constructive suggestion. They know, they really know, that they are absolutely ineffective as witnesses so long as they are outside the conversation. (Ineffective, that is, to relate to it; God can use many kinds of people to advance His purposes and they may be effective for other tasks.) Only when a person — in or out of a denominational group which "belongs" or does not belong — undertakes repentant and restorative action can he hope to commend Christ to the world which rejects Him because of a divided Church.

The burden of this attitude falls on well-meaning evangelicals who count themselves out of the ecumenical movement. Roman Catholicism is an actual participant in the conversation; Orthodoxy, at least as intransigent as Rome in its view of the perfect hold it has on the truth, is a full participant; many Protestant groups which tend to consider themselves and their autonomy of first importance are there. Are all of these participants there only for imperial reasons, to impose their whole existing nature on all others? Or do they see something in the make-up and assumptions of such conversation and shared work which has not yet been appropriated in evangelicalism? Since the evangelicals who are represented as observers or in the press are ordinarily quite responsive to what they see and hear, could it be that their supporting denominations stand off more out of habit and unexamined attitude than out of careful scrutiny of the conversation's basis?

"Why don't the churches get together?" It would be a delusion to think that this first question is anything more than a first question. The churches could "get together" and that act as such will not mean conversion of the world, acceptance of Jesus Christ, or interest in His works. (According to one account, a man followed all the advertiser's injunctions and got rid of his halitosis. He still did not gain friends.) The first question is merely the one which allows serious grappling with all the others. Satisfactory, positive answers to it might make possible the development of a Christian language which is again understandable in the public sphere. It might make a new theology possible.

Who shall bear the burden of answering the question? If it is put superficially by the "outsider" or the barely-inside Christians and profoundly by the professionally ecumenical, what about the rest of Christianity? Here it would seem that a basic failure of the churches is again concentrated. Jesuit Father John L. Thomas in his book *Religion and the American People* (Westminister, Maryland: Newman, 1963) has pondered the problem of American conformity to the names of Christian doctrines (Trinity, Divinity of Chirst, etc.) without corresponding curiosity concerning their meaning. He properly contends that not all church members can be expected to be equally informed or faithful. What has happened is that the churches have not developed a sufficiently broad elite of concerned and knowledgeable people.

This failure is patent on the ecumenical question. In many cases the energies of "pillar" members have been directed toward the housekeeping details of their own parishes or to the trivia of their denomination's life. Vital Christian energy is diverted from central concerns, and the "main stream" members often turn out to be least ready to face the seriousness of the world's question. Only when the question is really heard; only when its intent is made a part of the central discipline of church life; only when the ecumenical centrality of the general or pastoral prayers of the liturgy are accompanied by actions, will such an elite develop. Through the development of such an "elite" the broader membership of the church will be trained to convey to the world the reality of what has been going on unperceived by many for a half-century: the churches *are* getting together. They may not be doing it in the ways one might wish, but the direction of their lives are turned toward each other.

"Ecumenicity by public relations," someone once sneered when this mechanism was described to him. "Reunion of the Church through pseudo-events and manufactured images" is another charge brought against it. Cannot the guile of the serpent here be brought together with the innocence of the dove? If something has been happening in the churches, should they hide it under a bushel even when asked whether it has been happening? If they have enough unity to resume mission, is it illegitimate to say so?

Even the majority of the evangelical groups which have not committed themselves to the twentieth-century pre-occupation of most churches are able to give some sort of answer; whether they are willing to is the question. I refer to the fact that almost all Christian groups now formally, officially, publicly disavow proselytism — the attempt to manipulate conversions by using the membership of other churches as their prospect list and mission field. Desisting from proselytism has a logical and psychological corollary. If I do not enter a man's home and engage in proving to him that he is "unsaved" or, as the soap advertisers say, "half-safe" unless he breaks relations with his own church, I am asserting something positive. For if I have committed myself to the hope that salvation is in Jesus Christ and His truth, then — if I love my neighbor — I should make my view of truth prevail over alternative ones which he holds in Christ's name. If I do not, then I am suggesting that he is really "saved" or at least that being "half-safe" is enough for his good and to satisfy my sense of mission.

Christians do this "telegraphing of their shots" every day when they desist from proselytizing. When they *do* proselytize, they do so knowing that they are breaking more than "ground rules of the game." They are engaging in something theologically disdainful, alien to the nature of the Church. But both the logic and psychology of not proselytizing say that informal recognition of other Christian traditions and confessions goes on. Why should the churches not get credit for this quiet if negative way of asserting their almost universal understanding of the nature of the Church? We must surmise that they fail to develop theologies to correspond with the practice for two reasons: first, for short-range Christian missionary effectiveness it is more efficient to compete with each other. Since a theology for competition has no Christian rootage (it is based on purely pragmatic justifications), churches feel it advisable not to theologize about their practice too much. Second, to advertise the full meaning of their failure to proselytize might be misinterpreted (be careful to note that I did not say 'interpreted') as a casualness or indifference toward the fullness of Christian truth. In other words, there has been more readiness to teach justifications for competition than to undertake the pedagogical task of showing how one can see the Spirit of Christ formed in another with whom one does not fully agree, without weakening one's own serious hold on truth.

Here is the point of it all: if the Spirit of Christ is somehow formed in another person, be he Orthodox, Roman, Protestant of ecumenical or of evangelical bent, then I as a Christian am related to him in a unique way. It is a uniqueness of kind and not of degree, of quality and not of quantity. Recognizing the Spirit of Christ can never mean the last word of witness but only the basis for the first. It makes no sense in the New Testament's terms to stop edifying at the point where one begins. Christians are to exhort, to build each other up, to test their prophets and prophecies. But they do that *within the family*. They do it not by mere agreement over ground rules and etiquette but out of their heart of hearts and out of a profound and yet instinctive decision in the back of the Christian mind.

This practice of not proselytizing and its partly hidden logical corollary of quiet acceptance of other Christians is so obvious and so normal that it is seldom regarded for what it is: the theological basis for an answer to the question, "Why don't the churches get together?" The answer is: they are getting together because Christian people in the whole Church already are together. St. John Chrysostom's contention, quoted above, is correct: as there can be no interval between Head and Body, so there can be no separation between living members.

The twentieth-century effort to show forth Christian unity is an attempt to take on the burden of understanding this assertion, which will be the last word as it is the first, the maximum as it is the minimum, the fulfillment as it is the beginning of all our strivings.

Chapter Two

THE CONFUSION OF DIRECTIVES:
LOVE THY NEIGHBOR; SHOVE
THY NEIGHBOR

IF CHRISTIANS BELIEVE THAT CHRIST IS SOMEHOW FORMED in other Christians and if they take pains to recognize this formation, they are taking the first step toward recognizing their unity. As such, they possess enough unity to resume their mission. Conversely, mission resumed on the basis of mutual recognition will further enhance the cause of Christian unity. The proof? For a half-century and more it has begun to do precisely that. The Christian impulse toward mutual work and a common quest for the truth in Christ have been followed for more than a half-century in the ecumenical movement.

What has deterred the movement, once it began? Why does it often fail to capture the imagination and so often lapse into stalemate? The answer can be found in the lethargy of those who cling thoughtlessly to regional tradition, usually because they are remote from other traditions, or of those whose first attachment is to the denomination or sub-group of Christians to which they belong. The twentieth century, notorious for its complication of Christian mission and service and for its laying of obstacles in the path of faith and the language of faith, has not hampered Christian separatism. Attachment to the apparatus of denominationalism seems scarcely to have diminished at all.

The extent of this institutionalism is not difficult to measure, particularly in a nation like the United States. And of measurement we have plenty by sociologists and statisticians and opinion researchers. With wearying frequency they come back with the same conclusion. Most Christian energy is expended on the local or the denominational, on private or trivial concerns, on what serves to justify separation. The churches are beginning to tire of listening to this evidence, unfortunately before they have really heard it. Many a critic of church life must ask himself from time to time whether the critique of institutionalism is a philosophically or theologically profound theme. It all seems so obvious. Then his vocation calls him once more to study and reproduce his findings: denominationalism seems in no way to be hampered by secularism around and in the churches. It thrives on an environment where basic Christian questions are unasked and its forms seem to serve to justify half-believing men before God. This is the testimony of the church historians and sociologists of religion who are consistently puzzled by the growth of denominationalism in a century when its theological justification has begun to disappear; who are puzzled by the way ecumenism receives the leftovers in the century when its theological justification has newly appeared.

Quite clearly, ecumenical hopes cannot be pinned upon the complete death of denomination, tradition, or confession. Even were this death foreseeable, it is not sure whether the absence of these historic emphases would be an asset to the cause of Christian expression and unity. Therefore, since life comes only out of death, one must ask *what* in these separate causes must die. Their ability to hold the loyalties of people? The way they motivate people to teach, to sacrifice? Hardly. What must die is not what they *bring to* ecumenical reality but what has deterred their members *from* wholehearted participation. In most instances, what must die is the imperial spirit which refuses to examine the tradition and which seeks to pre-empt the present.

In this light the forms taken by the ecumenical movement of the twentieth century become understandable. They have been of two kinds, "conciliar" and "organic." The former refers to the federal principle of councils of churches, both local and international. In this principle churches keep separate identities but merge many of their concerns. The latter refers to the formation of a single churchly identity where there had been two. It will not be necessary here to detail all the steps along the way to the first or all the achievements of the second, but certain highlights may be cited.

One might picture the formation of a great stream. The longest course grows out of three sub-streams. One is the missionary emphasis which gave rise to the whole movement. Curiously, as an organization this emphasis did not merge with the others until 1961, over a half-century after it began to pour some of its resource into the larger movement. At two great international missionary meetings in the decades before World War II it became clear that an ecumenical missionary movement had no reason for separate life apart from the practical and theological concerns which paralleled it.

The second, practical stream is an emphasis called Life and Work which united Christian action into an impressive contribution. The third originating stream is Faith and Order, which in 1927, 1937, 1952, and 1963 met to keep the theoretical issues of disunity and unity before the churches. In 1948 the World Council of Churches was formed to incorporate missionary, practical, and theoretical emphases. The World Council of Churches has since met twice, including at New Delhi in 1961.

In the beginning practical concerns predominated. The Christians of the nineteenth century had responded to the challenges of modernity through practical action. For the most part, as the philosopher Alfred North Whitehead pointed out, they wavered in their appeal to constructive reason. The nineteenth-century habit of mind predisposed the ecumenical movement to works of love even where theoretical bases were lacking. The full story of these works has not yet made its way into public consciousness. The more profound threat to the Church, however, more profound than wars and ideologies, movements of people and ethical issues, was in the question of belief and thought. In the modern world great numbers of people seemed capable of living without God or "beyond God" and the basic claims of the Christian faith (to say nothing of the subtleties of traditions) were called into question.

All the while the growth of the non-Christian world was outstripping Christian growth. The original fire had gone out of the missionary movement. The offense of competition was being recognized by peoples "on the frontiers of the Christian world" who were becoming ever more sophisticated. The other great religions of the world were awakening from slumber. The real religion of the modern world, nationalism, preoccupied many. The secular spirit and a religious spirit devoted to vacuous generalizing were spreading. Most of all, population growth was greatest where Christians were least numerous.

To picture the confusion over missions we need not go so far as the theological question about what happens to the heathen who do not hear of Christ. This question will be raised in other contexts. If we keep within the confines of ordinary Christian concern for enlarging or seeing enlarged God's reconciling circle among men, we may yet see the difficulty (in the ecumenical half-century) imposed upon the "missionary century" which still lives on. It comes from two kinds of motivation being suggested to the same people.

On the one hand, the real "sap and passion" is removed from competition by the discouragement of proselytism and, even more, by the value attached to Christ's prayer for unity and Paul's picture of it. On the other hand, the whole apparatus of missions is directed toward competition and the enhancement of separation. Loyalties of people converge upon their own group as the charts and graphs of their independent successes are compared with the statistics of other Christians. Numbers of Christian groups crowd the same soil and implicitly undercut each other's work while large areas of the Western world, to say nothing of uncommitted elements of world population, are wholly neglected.

What should Christians do when they are caught between the command to co-operate and the practice of competing? Who can answer? We know, however, what they *did* do. They received the assets of neither directive and were burdened with the liabilities of both. They thought it illicit to exploit new populations vigorously. The relishing of Christian concord tempted them to relax their mission.

In a study of the political community Sebastian de Grazia has depicted this same phenomenon on a smaller scale. He calls it *anomie,* a listless normlessness in life, and traces it to a conflict in belief-systems when people receive conflicting "directives" from their rulers. The directives are "ways people believe they must act to avoid trouble, fear, and anxiety. From the positive side they are formulas for salvation or for success or for the good life." Fundamental to all the confusion has been conflict in directives between "love thy neighbor" and "shove thy neighbor." Other conflicts can help create *anomie,* among them the related one between activist and quietist diritives, but the competitive-co-operative tension is the most confusing. "So penetrating has been the competitive doctrine that it is difficult for most Americans to believe that life can be otherwise organized."[1]

The original charters of the ecumenical movements, which persist into the present, contribute to this problem. The

[1] Sebastian de Grazia, *The Political Community*: *A Study of Anomie* (Chicago: University of Chicago Press, 1948), pp. 47-59.

movement was born out of the co-operative directive of the Christian canon. But to be born, it had to guarantee the autonomy of member churches, and thus to license their competitive tendencies. De Grazia suggests that the political ruler who wishes to avoid *anomie* must decide between directives. Equally is this true in the churches. Quite obviously there is not a trace of biblical warrant for the competitive. This means that co-operation should rule the field. Yet, in the nineteenth-century mission, competition had served so well practically; is it conceivable that this should now be surrendered? This practice is sometimes justified in Christian circles by reference to American free enterprise.

Psychologically and practically much might he said for competition as a motive for mission and service. Historically, without question, it has had positive effects. But are not Christians people who are supposed to work from only one motive, and who are ready to suffer defeat rather than gain a victory from the wrong motivation? Take the example of the American suburbs of post-World War II. The new housing developments full of uprooted and semi-committed people provided "fair game" for representation by church extension boards of every subtle brand of denominationalism. The usual question was not: What place in America most needs a Christian presence? but Where can we fit in another representative of our denomination? This greediness did produce great numbers of churches, though there are evidences in the 1960s that popular disaffection for the pathetic scramble has understandably set in. At the same time, people of good will who wished to set up alternatives to competition were forced to devise traditionless and superficial "non-denominational churches." Lip service was paid to the ecumenical movement in the former circumstances through the practice of holding joint Thanksgiving services and co-operating in whichever other ways did not complicate denominationalism. Some sociologists have discovered that these pseudo-ecumenical ventures actually existed in many instances to justify a more ruthless kind of competition the rest of the time.

Asked to justify this kind of action, many extension boards would take one of two gambits. One set would point to the question of theological truth. Think of how many people in their hammocks and on their patios would be in terror of hell-fire if *we* were not an option in their midst. The more self-assured and crass would be purely practical: we get a return on our investment from the suburbs. This will come quicker through larger church organizations. These, in turn, will grow best if the "boys have to go out and scramble," keeping each other jumping. Indeed, for the minister and flock who could avoid the co-operative injunctions of the New Testament, the latter was a healthy-minded course. But for those in whom the ecumenical spark had taken fire, the confusion of directives was perplexing. We have spoken with many suburban ministers who were motivated to evangelize a community when it was really missionary soil. But when it came to be overchurched and the ministers and "calling committees" disgraced the Church by racing the milkmen to newcomers' doors, they withdrew and left the field to the competitive.

In the middle of the nineteenth-century Western New York State, after the experience of too many revivals of religion, was called a "burned-over district." It became a soil for popular lack of interest or for weird religious enthusiasms. The tapering off of the religious revival after about 1958 and the suburban attractions toward the quasi-religious political right wing around 1960 may be evidence that public instinct has again recognized a "burned-over district."

When one withdraws from missions or loses passion and fire but yet half-believes, is this the time to engage in ecumenicity? So it is sometimes portrayed. A study pamphlet at the World Student Christian Federation meeting at Strasbourg, France, in 1960 implied this accusation in a question: "When Christianity is vigorous, new churches spring up. Only in periods when faith is in decline do Christians speak about reunion. Discuss." And discuss it Christian people must. Is it only the failure of nerve of missionaries which produced the ecumenical movement? Was Pope John merely expressing Catholic defeatism when in 1959 he recognized Protestant-Orthodox ecumenism by setting up a secretariat for these matters; was he finding it necessary to join the sheep huddled in a storm, the mountain climbers who cling together to a rope over an abyss, when he convoked his own council?

These are the accusations of the missionary-oriented cynics, and of men of action who issue competitive directives in the Church, as well as the words of critics in the world who wonder why Christians must wait until the period of secularization to begin to notice each other. Perhaps some of this motivation may be involved. We have never heard of a reform being born in a settled social movement where there were no outside threats. At the same time, since it was missionary emphasis which gave birth to the ecumenical movement, one might more readily say that the Church which had "exhaled" in the nineteenth century found it necessary to "inhale" in the twentieth. After moving uncritically it was time to move self-critically.

Whoever argues for resumption of mission on the basis of the co-operative directive has to face the charge, which can be easily documented, that anti-co-operative groups grow more rapidly than do co-operative ones. Many considerations come into play here and we shall put them in question form: Should Christians "advance" on motivations which they know to conflict with New Testament and traditional Christian norms? Do the anti-ecumenical churches succeed because they are standoffish? Or are they anti-ecumenical and missionary because of some other feature which holds their life together? What about their second generation? Will they not, to consolidate gains, turn out to be more "institutional" and self-protective than the ecumenically banded-together churches? Most of all, are they not trading off deposits of good will which other Christians have prepared; and in the process of "snatching a few souls for salvation" actually complicating the wider and deeper work of Christians elsewhere and for the future? These questions may be answered with many subtle variations, yet their general direction is clear. At the same time, they should neither be asked nor answered in one way only to justify lethargy and apathy in churches which have sought to serve God in ways other than through immediate and dramatic conversions.

The *petite histoire* of the missionary, practical, and theological streams that went into the Protestant-Orthodox ecumenical councils and the Catholic merger of conciliar concerns need to be no more complete than this for our purposes. The reader who wishes historical detail may consult any number of books, notably Henry P. Van Dusen's *One Great Ground of Hope* (Westminster, 1961). Dr. Van Dusen presents a virtual day-by-day account of Christian Unity 1795-1960 in a chronology at the end of his book. Nor need we go into the task of citing the impressive number of actual mergers within and more recently across denominational lines. The churchly history of the half-century is profound witness to the ecumenical spirit of the time. The impulse has taken forms; but these forms — it must be remembered — also belong to the forms of the world which will be passing away. They need the kinds of criticism they are receiving today from — guess who? — students as rebels, laymen through impatience or alternate apathy, and missionaries and workers through criticism.[2]

---

[2] For the most complete sympathetic criticism of the World Council of Churches, to which I feel motivated to add nothing, see the symposium edited by Keith Bridston and Walter Wagoner, *Unity in Mid-Career* (New York: Macmillan, 1963).

This criticism is not chiefly of the "churchly" kind. The consensus of the critics of Roman Catholic and all other forms of ecumenicity seems to be that if the churches had the luxury to pursue their own ways apart from the world, the ecumenical movement would be seen to have "arrived." The alert criticism of today follows a different line. It is indifferent to the questions of ecclesiastical housekeeping and furniture placing. It is bored by details of council and merger. It is motivated by the widespread accent on what might be called a "theology for the world." This accent wants to take the Church into the arena and market place and factory; to represent a suffering Christ in the world's undergrounds; to forego the traditional favors shown the Church in the West. This emphasis asks, "Unity for what?" and is never content with answers which smell of dilettantism. It asks the Church to be at the side of the revolutionary and the sufferer, not merely reflecting but molding a new world. These questions impose a sense of mission on all forms of ecumenicity, a sense much more complex but no less urgent than those which gave birth to the movements toward unity a half-century ago.

Chapter Three

"THE ECUMENICAL MOVEMENT
HASN'T CAUGHT ON"

THE 1960s ARE THE YEARS WHEN ORGANIZATIONALLY THE ecumenical movement is knowing its greatest triumphs. The decade began with the meeting of the World Council of Churches for the first time on historically non-Christian soil at New Delhi in 1961, and moved on to a conference on Faith and Order at Montreal in 1963. The latter was distinguished by the fact that it survived, even though at last the cozily Protestant make-up of the movement was now dispelled by the presence of Orthodox from both sides of the Iron Curtain. The movement had produced its first popular figure of world-wide fame in Pope John XXIII, and its most publicized event, the Vatican Council, whose first sessions were held in 1962 and 1963. A Consultation on Church Unity met in 1962 and 1963 to consider eventual consolidation of energies of many Protestant groups in the U.S.A. Large families of denominations like the Lutherans were setting their houses in order through new mergers. World-wide confessional congresses like those of the Anglicans and Lutherans at Toronto and Helsinki in 1963 received due attention in headlines.

In the midst of the attention given this religious phenomenon in the public press and in the churches' leadership it may sound confusing to assert that "the ecumenical movement hasn't caught on" or to suggest that it is living on borrowed time and may soon pass from favor. It seems gratuitous to

48

suggest, further, that the movement's more difficult years are ahead. In professional athletics a "freshman" or "rookie" is observed closely in his sophomore year. A novelist is watched for his second book, an artist for his encore. The ecumenical movement certainly knew a magnificent triumph in coming into existence at all. It has succeeded in setting the terms by which the Church is measured from without and tends to prescribe the concerns also for anti-ecumenical forces in the churches.

The fascination does not go deep or wear long, however. The consolidation of ecumenical energies consumed a half-century, during which time the questions addressed to the Church began to change. Then: Which church bears the truth? Now: Is there anything to the whole business? The delayed fuse of nineteenth-century "death of God" talk is now exploding in the West. Anti-colonialism and the new nationalism coupled with the rebirth of other religions serve to place Christianity on the defensive and make it look like a product and servant of Western self-seeking. To meet the later set of questions addressed to men and women of faith, organizational interests will be secondary. The student movement of today is as iconoclastic and revolutionary in relation to ecumenical forms as its forefather was creative in setting them up.

While churchly concern goes into professional refinement of ecumenical organizations, something which we might call a "para-ecumenical movement" has come into being. This movement, perhaps without gratitude, takes for granted the ecumenical forms it inherited and is impatient with them. It regards them with mild interest. It lives off and trades off their capital and does not seek to compete by setting up alternate forms. It is disdainful in its attitude, however, toward the greatest enemy of the Church-unity movement: a self-directed localism.

This localism is the setting where one can properly say,

"The ecumenical movement hasn't caught on." Here is where a threat to established forms is perceived. Despite all the headlines and *Time* magazine covers, a reporter who would interview the leadership — to say nothing of the broad membership — of the typical Protestant congregation would be hard pressed to find someone who could name any of the "heroes or saints" or officers of Life and Work or Faith and Order or the World Council of Churches. Who has read any of the documents and joint statements issued to the churches? Who has pierced the denominations' invisible shield, by which ecumenical news is reported but in which it is secondary to localism in concerns?

When these questions are asked, one may rightfully question whether a certain romanticism is not being presupposed. Did the common people and the lay leadership in the nineteenth century feel involved in the missionary movements of that day? One can answer with some confidence, "Indeed, yes." Look at the hymns. Read the sermon illustrations, half of them conveying the romance of the remote. Read the letters of people; observe the make-up of voluntary and benevolent organizations. One may be suspicious of many motivations behind the fascination and involvement. Still, popular interest on any terms outstripped that of today. Why? We have no doubt that one reason was that people were given a *way* of feeling involved, were given something to *do*. "If you cannot preach like Paul," there was still plenty to do in support of missions. But as far as the ecumenical movement is concerned, what should be said? If you cannot administer like Visser 't Hooft or discuss like Edmund Schlink or report like Xavier Rynne, what is there to do? The response to the injunctions to pray, to pay attention, to think nice thoughts about ecumenicity, will soon wear thin. People may ooze good will toward the reunitive efforts, but they will not sustain this unless somehow it pierces the shield of professionalism and the barrier of localism.

Professional theologians and negotiators, of course, will do important work for many years to come and much of the movement's work will be carried on in conclaves that will, by being held at any given place, inevitably be remote from every other place. What is accomplished, then, is something that might be called "instant ecumenicity" or "ecumenicity by fiat." With all due respect for professional efforts toward perfection, this "progress" begins to live off the relative unity already reached and employs the movement's capital to "get back to work."

Practically, this is how matters tend to work out anyhow. The military chaplaincy never pretends that all its members agree theologically. It is not preoccupied with ecumenical ritual and the niceties of "joint worship services." It does what its situation demands. College chaplains, well aware of the dramatic effectiveness of denominational appeal "to keep their programs going," also learn more and more the importance of united Christian work if the campus and student are to be served. Any self-respecting theological conversation will be interdenominational in character and will not be self-conscious about it. No one asks the denomination of ministers in racial demonstrations or checks the credentials of the laymen who march.

Such people, however important it may be for them to certify their credentials with their sponsoring agencies, in effect are saying, "The ecumenical movement is far enough along," or, "It's already over," so far as the carrying on of their own activity is concerned. But these are all instances of churches at "boundary" situations where resources are thin and shallow. The moment the luxury of separation and competition is permitted, these are indulged in again.

"The ecumenical movement has not caught on." Today's world is more complex and Christian motivation is similarly more complicated than at the time when the missionaries' questions motivated reunion. The secular world shows a new potency. The coming generation is more critical. The local churches are so set up as not to have to pay much attention to churchly reunion. "The ecumenical movement does not sell," say the book publishers. "The people do not want ecumenicity," says my aging young friend in the employ of the movement, who has visited the churches and seen popular resistance based on the idea that ecumenicity means "giving things up."

Missions "sold," and to this day publishers can do well with derring-do tales of triumphs of the gospel over jungle primitivism. The people wanted missions, so long as they sensed superiority over the missionized. The people wanted ecumenicity so long as they thought it could be secured by the triumph of their forms over others. But to hear that the Church is today asked not to be triumphant but to serve quietly; that it exists not for superiority but for suffering; that ecumenicity does not mean regrouping for imperial goals — these mean the death of self. Who would expect that idea to "sell" or to "catch on"?

There is no immediate prospect of the ecumenical reality becoming vivid in the minds of Christians so long as the theology of the movement is preoccupied with churchiness (ministry, orders, polity, etc.). Nor will it incarnate human desires if it has to coexist with the more vivid competitive directives in the denominations or with the commanding loyalites of localism. Most of all, it cannot become central in Christian thought so long as two of its three shaping tendencies are played off against each other. This point must be detailed.

A person who had a blank piece of paper and was asked to chart a "way out" of the maze of Christian division in 1910 could with perfect logic have sketched approximately what did happen. He would have been asked for missionary reasons. Immediately, however, he would have confronted the two great poles of ecumenical thought. The one came to represent the co-operative directive of shared work which, in the World Council of Churches' instance, was the original Life and Work movement. This tendency represented "instant ecumenicity" in its day. Men of good will were presumed to be capable of attempting great things in the world for Jesus Christ's sake without coming to agreements on theology. Life and Work by itself could have become mere altruism had it not been balanced by other forces.

The organizational pole of "other forces" was the Faith and Order movement (1927ff., though the first stirrings occurred around 1920). Faith and Order was, of course, oriented toward theology and church order. From the first and down through Lund (1952) it had to content itself with "comparative ecclesiology" as a method. This is a fancy way of saying that when ecumenical churchmen gathered they would begin by asserting what their tradition represented and what they understood others to represent. The gatherings would conclude with a report of these comparisons with special reference to the consensus arrived at by this method. The consensus grew out of several approaches. First, there would be removal of misunderstandings between the churches because of private languages and separate histories. Then would follow a "smoothing over the rough bumps," that is, an attempt to let the central point of each tradition's emphasis stand and to let the edges be worn away in the light of the experience of the whole Church. Third, a new light on the tradition itself would be gained through common study of the Bible and Christian history. During the 1950s the Faith and Order Commission produced a rather remarkable document on Baptism by this method.

The accent on Faith and Order was, of course, different from that of Life and Work. In place of the co-operative directives of "instant ecumenicity" there was the permanent assurance that no one's autonomy of organization or tradition or opinion was threatened unless he chose it to be. Comparative ecclesiology as a method can be construed as a fine postgraduate course in the doctrines of the separate churches. It represented "permanent autonomy." Implied, of course, is the competitive directive. The formation of the World Council of Churches and the greater participation of Roman Catholicism — which has had to be on the basis of faith and order — has enhanced this directive.

Christian people, therefore, are confronted with a co-operative *versus* competitive directive at the very heart of the efforts toward reunion. Faith is always a fragile and tender plant; it can easily wither. Interest in the affairs of the Church must always compete with the apparently more vivid concerns of personal and social life in the world; not much incentive is needed to let weak faith combine with apathy in church affairs. Christian people need all the help they can get in the stimulation and sustaining of their imaginations if the whole condition of Christ's Church in the world is to be regarded. When the first frail interest and the first real participation in matters ecumenical are evidenced in any Christian, he is confronted with the confusion of directives. He hesitates, is bewildered, and confused. As the complexity of ecumenical concerns becomes vivid he cancels himself out. "Life and Work" he relegates to organizations set up for benevolent purposes. "Faith and Order" he turns over to professional theologians and thus abandons. From time to time he may show passing interest in dramatic events of ecumenism (the Vatican Council) or in an occasional commanding personality of the world-wide Church. But he soon lapses into the affairs (at best) of localism and denominational loyalism of the church and (at worst) of selfish pursuits in the world. "The ecumenical movement hasn't caught on" for another person.

Realistically, he should not be blamed. To be told that he can participate by showing interest and praying, but that is all, is the same as being told that he should not participate at all. Who can sustain permanent interest in the organizational detail of even the most selfless organization? Who can sustain an imagination over a technical conversation in which his presence is implicit but in which he has no promise of participation? Yet the logic of the diagram of ecumenical organization is evident. "Instant ecumenicity" had to be represented to initiate the conversation; "permanent autonomy" had to be promised in order to build confidence in the conversation. What is forgotten in the playing off of these tendencies is the original commanding motif: the mission of the Church. *It* pulled people into their basic concern to work together and to find each other; it constantly slips from view in ecumenical thinking and activity.

Bit by bit and piece by piece, as organic mergers of denominations and regional churches occur, it might be argued that the problem will solve itself. It is presumed that merged churches will automatically enlarge the sphere of ecumenical service within their enlarged borders. It is similarly presumed that, merger having occurred on the basis of theological agreement, the competitive directives will be minimized. To a certain but still unsatisfying degree this is so. But the charter of ecumenism remains: as *councils* the ecumenical groups insure co-operation; as councils of *churches* they guarantee implied competition. A conservatism has been built into Protestant-Orthodox ecumenism which will inevitably be deepened as Roman Catholicism enters the picture. "Faith and Order" is structurally exhanced and upgraded at the very moment when its conversation becomes most complex and frustrating within Protestantism and Orthodoxy. The "Protestant-Catholic dialogue" exaggerates the problem by further removing the experience of church reunion from laymen and the local parishes and further relegating it to the professionals and hierarchies of church life. Once again: "The ecumenical movement has not caught on"; it has not affected the day-to-day life of people in the local situations of Christianity.

Let us attempt to view, once more, the conflict of directions and directives so long as mission is neglected. This time picture the interest in co-operation and "instant ecumenicity" as being a centripetal force in church life. The sheep were huddled in the storm. The falling climbers grasped at one rope. The inhabitants of the shadow world clutched at each other to find their way through the fog. The separated members of a family rejoiced at being reunited even though they had not settled their family problems. This emphasis was centripetal, incarnated in what Jesuit Father Gustave Weigel usually calls the "union now" school of thought. This centripetal impulse, of course, is easiest to sustain when the base of church participation is as narrow as possible. It is easiest to promote when "main-stream Protestantism" is implied; matters are complicated when "fringe Protestantism" must be regarded. They are still more to be frustrated when Orthodoxy with its doctrine of the Church enters. They become almost hopeless when Roman Catholicism with its hierarchical insistence has to be reckoned with. The last plausible assertion of this somewhat cozy view of the movement is represented in an essay by Charles Clayton Morrison, "Protestantism Is Ready *Now* to Become One Church." His theses, reprinted in reports of the Oberlin North American Conference on Faith and Order of 1957, deserve quotation as being most representative of this view:

> A. We are all agreed that the members of all our churches are Christians, equally accepted by Christ as members of his Church.
> B. All our denominations are by intention, conviction and in fact equally Christian churches.
> C. All our denominations share equally in the sin of maintaining schismatic churches.
> D. Our way of thinking about the Christian faith has undergone profound changes in the past half century.
> E. The doctrinal differences which formerly existed between the denominations are now embraced in the denominations themselves.

F. Our denominations are now beginning to see that their differences, such as they are, can be more hopefully reconciled within a united church than in sectarian isolation.

G. The association of our denominations in national and community federations has led them into a mode of co-operation which is, in principle, organic.[1]

Dr. Morrison's development of these theses is informed, impassioned, compelling, and eloquent. It represents the "last best hope" of the "union now" school of reunion. But it is not being widely argued today, years later. Why? The answer lies in the theses themselves.

Only one of the theses, the first, is demonstrably theological, rooted in the Bible and belonging to the agreed-upon tradition of the churches. All those who are members of the churches are Christians — if they are believers in Christ and found in Him. Then, of course, they are and have to be equally accepted by Christ as members of His Church. Otherwise in fact there would be an interval between Head and Body. Otherwise there would have to be a denominational tag on the "members of the body" which represent the hands and legs and heart as opposed to the weaker or humbler or less attractive members. (Picture the unlovely competition if each denomination were asked to describe *which* part of the Body in this symbolism *it* represented!)

However, Dr. Morrison's first thesis being granted, what of Orthodoxy and Roman Catholicism? The members of these churches "are Christians, equally accepted by Christ as members of his Church." But after this thesis is thus asserted, the other six are not recognized. Othodoxy cannot *not* be included in a movement that claims to be ecumenical, and yet it does not agree with much of anything at all in these theses. Roman Catholicism is in the same situation. If Protestants represent 28% of the 28% of humanity that is

---

[1] *Christian Unity in North America: A Symposium,* edited by J. Robert Nelson (St. Louis: Bethany, 1958), pp. 150ff.

named Christian (I speak as a statistical fool!), and if allowance be made for the majority of Protestantism which does not follow or act upon the other six theses, Dr. Morrison's ecumenical movement would tend to become a very anti-ecumenical club. The introduction of Orthodoxy and Roman Catholicism into the conversation flowed inevitably and followed integrally from the logic of the Christian's first assertion about the nature of the Church. But the actual presence of Orthodoxy and Roman Catholicism dashed the hopes of the "union now" people and revealed them to be part of a private vision, however admirable that vision might have been!

Since "union now" cannot win, "truth first" has its claims enhanced. Its first thesis is no less compelling in its logic or theology than was the "union first" thesis. That is, no expression of Christian unity deserves the adjective "Christian" unless it is grounded completely in the truth in Jesus Christ and unless it be judged at all times from the viewpoint of the quest for that truth among churches and church people. Here again, one can point to remarkable evidences of growing consensus. Dr. Morrison actually does so in one of his theses: that reconciliation of differences must occur, but that it occurs best after union. No one can deny that reconciliations on the ground of Christian truth have occurred in the organic mergers of denominations after theological agreement and in the growing consensus within "main-stream Protestantism."

"Truth first," however, as a slogan paralyzes ecumenical work and becomes a wholly unrealistic basis for witness if by that is meant: we cannot do anything together to show forth the works of love and to speak the words of judgment and grace in Christ until the organizations and denominations and churches produce committees which can produce documents which can be agreed upon by the various members of all the churches. (This is the implied approach of the organizationally-oriented proponents of "truth first.") There is no possibility for a "daily plebiscite" or a universal ballot among all the members of the Church to express their agreement on the truth in every detail. Therefore, if this assumption is followed, the actual work and expression of efforts toward reunion and worship are wholly delegated and relegated to professionals and committees and commissions. When this happens, "the ecumenical movement hasn't caught on." When this happens, one becomes ecumenical by belonging to the organization which establishes the conversation. He is justified by belonging to an institution whose representatives participate in interdenominational talk. Patently, this is an absurd if not blasphemous twist on the New Testament's injunctions to seek unity in the Church. Christian people who recognize this and therefore reveal their apathy and go about other business should be congratulated for their insight into the gospel, an insight unmatched among those who, in a technical world, look for salvation in the proceedings of technical religious organizations.

"Truth first" as a slogan runs into trouble also in the actual attempts of the past half-century. While profound agreements between Christians exist, Protestantism remains divided and Orthodoxy and Roman Catholicism are nowhere in range of each other or of Protestantism. If one must wait for documentary agreement and organizational realignment, one whole dimension of the biblical command and promise concerning the Church will be cut off from Christian view and profession. "Truth first": by itself this slogan denies some elements of the doctrine of the Church while affirming others. It can only be centrifugal. It guarantees, in the hands of those who wish to misuse it, the privileges of autonomy and the priorities of selfishness and pride.

Has the ecumenical movement worked itself into a corner? Has this report magnified an argument which should be minimized, hidden, pushed into a corner? Indeed, yes, if the "truth first" *versus* "union now" or the centrifugal over against

the centripetal or the competitive *versus* the co-operative directives are correct ways to state the fundamental issue. If
it is correct, then one should at once assert not that there
are varieties of gifts but the same spirit, but rather that there
are two spirits. It would be better then that there be two
ecumenical parties or movements. Churches or people should
be asked to choose one or the other as the only escape from
confusion and its resultant apathy and *anomie*. Each of these
parties could be clear, direct, simple. Each could summon
energy and passion. Each would have a clear sense of direction. The two ecumenical movements would "catch on."
Obviously this version of the ecumenical intention is impossible to hold within the Christian claim. The fault,
therefore, must be in the way of stating the problem.

The fault lies in the word or the assumption "first." This
assumption establishes a competition which is "uncatholic":
that is, it lacks wholeness. It arrogates to man what belongs
only to God: the assured knowledge of the path to unity.
Unity there must be and truth must be. But unity already
exists: it remains to be discovered. Truth is in Christ: Christians are to be found in Him. Any version of ecumenism
which plays these off against each other will lead to confusion
and *anomie*. The creative Christian will join the self-directed
institutionalist in saying, "Count me out." The former will
do it because he knows that neither union nor truth can come
first as either goal or strategy. The latter will do so because
he enjoys his own world, with the luxury of disunity and
lack of interest in exposing "his" truth to discussion. Each
will give mild notice to the world's question, "Why don't the
churches get together?" Each will read, with differing re-
actions, the newspaper accounts of ecumenical progress and
regress. But in the mind and heart of both, the ecumenical
movement "has not caught on." Is there, then, a more
excellent way?

Chapter Four

THE UNITY WHICH DIVIDES US

IN THE PREVIOUS CHAPTER WE TRIED TO PICTURE TWO tendencies which conflict in ecumenicity. The "union now" advocates are few and far between today. Those who hold the position usually are at the edges of the movement, or are halfheartedly involved in church life, or they have not been exposed to the difficulties of providing the plan of union. The experience of Christians in the past two centuries has suggested that those who run around with a plan for universal Christianity in their hip-pockets ordinarily carry the most private and partial visions. On the other hand, the "truth first" emphasis is fruitless. It divides what the Scriptures unite. It sets theologically and psychologically unrealistic goals. It takes a quality of the life of the Church which belongs only to God and His last word, and wants it to become the Church's first word. Inevitably the "truth first" movements become stalemated or skewed from their goals.

What of the future, in a time of impatience over the two basic approaches to church unity? The "union first" emphasis inspires a party which argues that Christians dare not settle into a pattern of permanent disunity. The "truth first" school can show that Christian unity built on truthlessness or lack of interest in truth contributes nothing consistent with the Church's charter. Whoever looks for a way out of the ecumenical stalemate has to begin by looking into the forms of Christian life which now receive attention in the Church.

61

Remember: the argument of this book is that Christians now possess enough unity to resume mission, after a self-conscious and inward-directed period of churchliness. If that is so, it becomes necessary to locate the offense to the world in the current relation of church to church as well as the barriers to Christian imagination which the situation produces. The offense will be found within the kinds of unities which Christians now possess, namely, in their confessions, traditions, and denominations.

The first and best kind of unity, namely the organic, full, agreed-upon union of all Christians, is not in sight. At the other extreme, the disintegrative, partial, contentious life of the Christian individual apart from the Church comes under severe Christian judgment. Christians are in fact neither all together in a visible and public way, nor are they privately going each in their own way, each a threat to the throat of the other. They move between these impossibles. They unite in various ways to confess, to experience, to work.

The first form of existing unity can be summarized under the term *confessional*. When people gather to profess their faith, to unite in proclaiming it, to give substance to its stated and visible life among men, they form confessing churches. Thus the confessing group and its symbols serve to call believers out of isolation and anarchy into the beginnings of coherence and shared life. A confession serves to define and thus to delimit the boundaries of belief and shared life. It appears at a moment in the churches' lives and in response to specific needs and questions. Thus the confession is an event related to the tradition of the church. The confessional reality can, therefore, be spoken of as a "unity which divides," for at the moment that it unites it serves to rule out some past Christian experience and some present forms of expression. It is necessary to relate this confessional reality on the one hand to the ecumenical core of Christian life, and on the other to the more divisive expressions. The distinction between forms of Christian life and loyalty should be made in the light of the kinds of priority they should receive and do receive in day-to-day life. What is the offense in each form? What has to be changed or corrected to make more visible the Christian mission?

The term "confession" or "confessionalism" is encountered far more frequently in the ecumenical era than in the period of intense competition which preceded it. When Christians lived in geographical and personal isolation; when their attitude toward other Christians was based on ignorance or simple suspicion, the confessional reality was obscured. When social forces push divided parts of the Church closer together or when common action pulls them together it becomes necessary to define the separate partial visions of the Christian wholeness. Here we can account for the revival of confessionalism.

Take some simple, concrete instances. Methodism and Anglicanism in England shared a common history and were drifting into closer relations about the time the formal ecumenical movement was being born. Perhaps they might have been on the verge of a union based on memory, time-healed wounds, practical necessity, and broadly-based theological unities. In some respects each lived an unexamined life.

The international missionary conferences; the gatherings for study of Life and Work or Faith and Order; the increase of communication in a shrinking globe — these served to make British Anglicans more aware of their bond with those in India, the United States, and elsewhere who shared their "confession." Soon Methodists were finding at these gatherings that as Christians, if not as nationals, they were more at home with Methodists outside Britain than with Anglicans in it. They felt most constrained to come to better understanding with their "separated brethren" in their immediate family before they began to get to know their distant cousins. As they met and renewed acquaintance they found it necessary to examine the family and study its current patterns of authority. The movements were oriented toward family history and toward the practical affairs of ordering family life. Thus a peculiar and apparently self-contradictory form of ecumenism took shape: confessionalism. The broader the quest, the more precise the findings; the more widely based the effect, the narrower was the reality. In the attempt to address others, each family first had to explore its own mind and heart.

Whoever has attended a family reunion of any of these world-wide confessional families will have experienced a form of ecumenicity which is at once heart-warming and disturbing. Arguments seem more heated because they occur between people who have to get along more than do those who come from separate families in separate houses. On the other hand, cheering evidences of Christian love are also present. The souvenirs are set forth on the tables; the family albums are opened; the old songs are sung lustily. While the arguing and agreeing go on, however, the observer experiences a deepening feeling that the growing profundity of life in this particular family may also prevent its members from caring about others. Confessionalism was a necessary transitional phase of the ecumenical movement. Some of what it stands for will remain as a parallel to the whole ecumenical concern. But confessionalism also represents part of the offense of division.

All over the Christian map these confessional families have joined forces: the Lutherans in 1923 and 1947, the Presbyterian and Reformed in 1877, the Baptists in 1905, the Methodists in 1881, the Anglican after 1867, the Congregationalists in 1891. While most of these dates precede Edinburgh 1910, they represent some of the waxing ecumenical spirit first fully revealed at Edinburgh, and the on-going like of the confessional parties was deepened only in the light of inter-confessionalism after Edinburgh.

In what ways is confessionalism part of the offense to the world and a denial of the nature of the Church? Confessing as an activity for Christians certainly is not! Confessing is not saying, "This you have to believe," but rather, "This I believe," or, "This we believe." In some form or other, clear or unclear, timid or courageous, pure or impure, confessing is as natural as breathing for Christians. To confess means to take a stand, to find a coherence for faith, to give form to the basic grasp of reality. To confess means to define what the faith is not, or to suggest what is not important to it. It seeks to divide truth from falsehood, to suggest what a man affirms and what he denies, what he will die for and what he will concede.

The partiality of the confessing act among the confessions is most evident to those of different confession. The partisan of the Westminster or Augsburg Confession is tempted to see his own as a full and final expression of Christian truth; it forms a tent under which he presumes all biblical evidence and all Christian experience can be gathered. At the base of the Westminster Confession is a view of God's majesty which is not denied or contradicted by other groups. When it receives first emphasis, however, all the other assertions of faith become its corollaries in a unique way. At the heart of the Augsburg Confession is an understanding of God's grace which is not necessarily denied or contradicted by others. But when it is the first word, the keynote and *Grundmotif* or basic motive, all the other assertions which radiate from it will appear to be somehow different than in the heritage of Westminster. Neither is, then, a full and final expression. Each belongs to events and experiences owned by a *part* of the Church. Each, by what it affirms most emphatically, inevitably de-emphasizes other matters. Each provides a unity for great numbers of Christians; but each divides from others.

A confession serves to mark the Christian from the secular,

the specifically Christian from the generally religious, the particular Christian vision from the undefined one. Its words, when affirmed in writing or speech, produce a visible and definable community over against which the enemies of the Church can take their position. The confessing character of the Church guarantees that it be no "Platonic community" or abstraction. In all of these senses there are no confessionless churches. (The term for the reality is not important.) There may be churches of inarticulate or articulate confessions, of undisciplined or disciplined confessional life; there may be churches where the assertion of grasped truth is what defines the gathering and others where it is a secondary feature. But to say "Church" is to speak of a responding community and thus to speak of "confession."

So long as there are numbers of confessions in the world, however, confessions divide the Christian whole even as they unite the parts. All Christians are explicitly or implicitly of one confession or another; there are no "Church Citizens No. 1" even as in international affairs there was no place for a "World Citizen No. 1." Such is the nature of man, including Christian man, that his corporate life becomes self-directed as readily as does his personal self. The act of confessing separately is a complication in the shared life. The relation between the Christian's life inside the ecumenical reality (the Church is already one) and inside the confessing fellowship (its parts profess their faith in various ways) is intricate. Obviously the former takes priority in the Christian scheme. There can be no love, no communication across confessional lines unless there is this prior commitment to the oneness of the Church. Unless this is the first word spoken, there will be as many churches as there are confessions and as many confessions as there are individual men. But "if any man be in Christ, he is a new creature." The new creature's breach with the past and his hold on the new reality are of such a kind that his relation to *all* others found in Christ differs in kind from those who do not confess Christ's name.

The attachment to the core reality, the ecumenical assertion of Christian oneness, does not seem to be very "functional" in inter-church affairs. For the confessions do not only grasp positively at Christian truth. In defining and delimiting the confessing assembly they may or must speak out against those versions of Christian truth which they feel to be wrong. This is problematic particularly in the case of Orthodoxy, which denies to other bodies the definition "Church" in the full sense of the term. It is a problem in the instance of Roman Catholicism because of its consolidation of authority in a hierarchy headed by the Supreme Pontiff as Vicar of Christ. This is a confession which makes one a Roman Catholic; for the Protestant to confess it would mean the end of his Protestantism.

The presence of these variant confessions may remain until the end-time. It is difficult to envision a Church on earth which has eliminated all substantial differences; fulfillment of reunion is an "eschatological" hope. That is, its completion belongs to the activity of God and the end of history. The Christian has and hopes. His hope, however, is "projected backward" into history. He is to work in history for the coming of the Kingdom or, better, for man's awareness of its nearness and presence. That Kingdom presupposes and produces the community called the Church. Letting this "hope projected backward" become a vivid part of the lives of Christian people demands the first energies of all clergy and laity. Neglect of this task of recognition would mean that members of the Church are only "playing games" and letting their highest calling dissipate into trivia.

In actual experience it is clear that more energy is expended in the refinement of confessions than in the recognition of the one Church. There are many obvious psychological reasons for this. The confession provides a place to stand to view the world. It offers a means of organizing experience into a coherent whole. It keeps Christian words from eroding into polished generalities or relativities. What is "hot" and what is "cold?" To people on the Equator "hot" means something different than it does to someone emerging from an igloo. What is "fast" and what is "slow"? The company of four-minute mile runners thinks differently of speed than does the company of paraplegics. Confessions reproduce "hot" or "cold," "fast" or "slow" as they are perceived by a specific company of people who share a particular history. Because the history is shared, people are drawn together. No wonder that more loyalties are extended to the partial than to the total!

The psychological tendency to attach to the particular and the local is even more evident in the second kind of existing unity, which we are here calling *tradition.* "Tradition" here does not mean what it is coming to mean in ecumenical talk: the *traditum* or act of handing over by God of His own life to His disciples and to the Church. Here it means more the *traditiones,* the traditions of men which gradually come to be seen to be integral to faith as confessions are. Traditions in this sense, however, are not integral. They can strengthen the hold of the man of faith on faith. They can also become his idols and images, his comfortable gods. Because of their color, texture, richness, and nearness these traditions can take on some of the character of household gods.

Traditions also make up elements of Christian life which we can call "unities which divide." The church without a sense of tradition is itself not a unified gathering. It is made up of atoms, of individuals who are related to each other casually and as tangents and not with the vital centers of their lives. But since these traditions are in every sense private and particular — indeed, they define privacy and particularity — they serve to divide Christian from Christian. Traditions of this sort will also belong to the Church until the end-time. Few are more tyrannized by tradition than are those who claim to be traditionless. An announcement on the bulletin of a radical campus says, "The following tradition goes into effect next Tuesday. . . ." A mission church in its second year finds itself bound by the traditions of the single usage of the year before. Such is the nature of man and of persons in relation to each other that they must constantly fabricate images in rhythm and for repetition.

Traditions have less theological validity than do confessions; they should come under more severe scrutiny since they so readily become idols. But as a psychological or esthetic product they are inevitable and necessary. I have often pictured the complex of tradition as one which serves as a cuticle. As the body grows a cuticle, an outer skin, so does the corporate Body of people. If every nerve had to be responsive to every external impulse a man would soon lose his sanity. The protection of the cuticle serves to filter or organize experience.

The validity of tradition is best seen when it is removed. The Chinese Communist "ant heap" communes served to disrupt people from rootage and tradition and thus to rob them of personhood. Prison wardens know the importance of permitting the development of tradition for the sake of morale. Human art and artifact grow out of the traditional community. As such, tradition becomes a handmaiden of the Word of God in ministering to faith. If one visits a Scottish Presbyterian Church and finds that it contrives to be ecumenical by expressing itself in Negro spirituals, one feels cheated, dislocated. The Bach *B Minor Mass* as an element of a Sunday morning service in a white wooden Methodist church in Iowa seems to be a temporary and artificial transplant. We can be quite sure that Anglican worship would be impoverished were it robbed of the Prayer Book tradition. The town-meeting character of some Congregational churches is a human tradition that survives and must survive in an era of complex organizations unless an element of authenticity is to be lost.

Traditions divide. A Rouault painting, part of the experience of the Western Church in its understanding of Jesus Christ the Suffering Servant, seems blasphemous at worst and meaningless at best to the Eastern Christian. Yet is not there validity of an ecumenical character in his exposure to the private tradition of another part of the Church? Cannot a Western Christian, brought up on the vision of the tortured human Christ and His sorrowful mother, see an enrichment of his spiritual life as he comes to know the meaning of an Eastern icon in which the Christ of Glory appears? Patient and empathic contact between Christians can mean a cross-fertilization of Christian regions and experiences. It need not lead to cross-sterilization and barrenness. Why should the ecumenical movement usually be described as an impoverishment of tradition instead of an enlargement? Why is it often portrayed as reduction instead of addition, leading to less rather than more? Still, the experience of the Church in so many times and places is so rich and varied that it inevitably serves also to divide. Since more energy is devoted and more loyalty extended to the particular and local, one may again say that attachment to tradition often occurs at the expense of attachment to the ecumenical reality and cause.

If this be true in the green tree of tradition, what of the dry tree of denominationalism? If tradition can be spoken of as a cuticle which gathers experiences and develops privacy, *denominationalism* (the third kind of existing unity) does so even more. Denomination includes an element of accident. Few details of anything particular about a denomination are dictated or anticipated by the Scriptures or Christian tradition. A denomination represents a necessary adaptation to modern complex organizations and a technical society. It is a peculiar modern creation of a practical nature. The presence of a number of confessions and gathered traditions in a specific nation or region demanded the development of a new form of religious organization. Modern pluralism, the expression of religious freedom in an open and neutral society, calls forth the denomination as a voluntary creation. Denomination is related to tradition as clothing is to cuticle; tradition is related to confession as skin to mouth; confession to ecumenical expression as mouth to heart. Denominationalism patently divides Christians, commanding their first loyalties.

Not everything about the denominational accident is evil because it is arbitrary. If one accepts the terms of a pluralist society and is alive to what history gives man in any generation, he must today accept denominationalism and deal with its varieties. But — and most denominationalists are being dragged screaming into this awareness — the price one pays for this is the lessening of seriousness with which men take the Christian expression of truth.

> The basic contention of the denominational theory is that the true Church is not to be identified in any exclusive sense with any particular ecclesiastical institution. The outward forms of worship and organization are, at best, differing attempts to give visible expression to that larger life of the whole Church which embraces all Christians. Thus no denomination claims to represent the whole Church of Christ, nor does it regard all other Churches as false Churches. On the contrary, all denominations expect to cooperate in freedom and mutual respect with other denominations in discharging their common responsibilities to God and the world.[1]

The denominationalist among Christians has a higher view of denominationalism than this and the "outsider" has a lower one. The denomination is basically a sociological category. The bland neutrality of the name itself is an indicator! Truman Douglass has spoken for the ecumenical conscience when he spoke of denominationalism as the "un-

[1] Winthrop Hudson, "American Protestantism," in *Crossroads,* VII, 29.

critical assumption that the denomination and its enterprises are proper objects of ultimate loyalty."

The ecumenical complication of denominationalism and localism can be deduced from almost every social scientist's study of American religious institutions. Gerhard Lenski in *The Religious Factor* (Doubleday, 1961), while he set out to learn something else about metropolitan religion, turned up significant evidence concerning how opinions are formed and loyalties nurtured in religious institutions. The ecumenical reality and its theological center are barely visible in popular religious expression. The confessional impulse is minimized. Local tradition is enlarged unrealistically in the imagination. Overpowering in the production of opinion and notion is the experience of the sub-community and the local cell. Thus a member of the bowling team of a First Methodist Church is more likely to draw his conclusions concerning the political or economic meaning of faith from the opinions of his fellow bowlers than he is from the Methodist tradition, the confessional experience of Wesley, or the theological center of the New Testament canon.

Denominations are defended as a means of safeguarding Christian truth; in actual effect, however, they serve to advertise Christian differences. They place truth on a cafeteria line. They call the world's attention to the relativity and competitive character of truth. They render trivial difference permanent and major. Denominationalism works against itself theologically, however practically inevitable it may now be.

Any Christian who has read the periodicals of his denomination or who has participated in the program of the church will be well aware of the temptation there presented to regard the world inside the denomination as the real world and the status it confers to be real status. Fortunately the ecumenical movement has begun to serve as a check on this tendency and from time to time a denomination may forego many of its privileges and understate its claims for the sake of the whole Church. Since the denominational is the most efficient, best organized, most secular and adaptable expression of corporate Christian life, it can appeal most powerfully to the sense of "the old school tie" that unites men into close bonds. But of the four kinds of gathered life (the first being full organic unity of all Christendom), denominations produce the kind of unity which divides most radically.

Fortunately, while "clothes make the man" insofar as visibility is concerned, they do not exhaust what he represents among those who take patience to pierce to his heart. Thus within the accident of denominationalism and under the cuticle of tradition there is a real communication of the mind and heart of Christian love that crosses the barriers produced by men and their history. But this communication is the least visible and most unreal of all Christian expression to the "outsider" or the fringe member. Only by a consistent act of will and a constant summoning of energy can Christians reverse their instinctive tendency, which is to devote themselves most to that which divides while leaving the energies of the end of the day or the bottom of the budget or the least vivid prayer to the common expression of Christ's presence in Church and world.

This book is not written as a primer in foolishness or as a manual of dreams. As such, it is not setting forth a way of finding unity by removing denominations. Precisely the opposite: it seeks a means of showing forth unity in spite of denominationalism and during the era of denominations. Numbers of movements to form non-denominational Christianity in America during the past century have inevitably succeeded in adding one more denomination. The denominationalism of the self-consciously "non-denominational" postwar suburban church is often more stifling and conformist than historic denominationalism. One may hope and work for the immediate end of denominations. He may drag his feet in reluctance to co-operate with their history; he may withdraw consent from the overpowering loyalties they would assemble. Social forces from without and Christian re-formation from within may be causing the end of the denominational period, and ultimate Christian survival and renewal may very well depend upon it. But the way to work for fresh Christian mission through united presentation of Christ is not through idle dreaming about *beginning* such work when denominationalism *ends*.

> Christ cannot any longer be proclaimed in a competitive situation. In a world of rapid social change can we lose the sense of urgency faced with the world to be evangelized? Can we forget the billion and a half of non-baptized in Asia and the 170 million of Africa? While we are advancing in scattered ranks the world is fashioning itself without us. Christians, by a deplorable competition that they set up among themselves in the same missionary locality, sometimes use up the best of their energy in condemning or in neutralizing each other. Some go to preach the Gospel where Christ is already proclaimed (perhaps because thus they justify in their own eyes their confessional position as well-founded). By such action Christians are forgetting the swift evolution of the world and are in danger of soon being submerged under a thousand fathoms of water in little local churches without any visible unity between each other.
>
> Now if there is no fellowship — and competition does away with any kind of communion — the radiance of the Gospel is compromised in the eyes of all those who are unable to believe.
>
> Of course we shall not end up by leading the whole world to explicit faith. But as we wish the world to fashion itself with us we believe it is necessary to seek to regain our unity first of all and to make of the quest for visible unity an indispensable prelude for Christian mission faced with a world which cannot believe.
>
> While we wait for this visible unity there still remain for our missionary thrust so many vast regions where Christ is not proclaimed. In such places these little households of Christians can go and become agents of transfiguration. On

such households of light, scattered throughout the world, by secular institutes, or under some other form of community, depends the very hope for the civilization to come. These households will take on the non-believing world. In the same way as, according to the apostle, the unbelieving husband is sanctified by the believing wife, so the world which is unable to believe, is adopted, transfigured by some Christians, who are Christ-bearers. However, it is still necessary to provide for this sort of presence.[2]

---

[2] Roger Schutz, *Unity Man's Tomorrow* (New York: Herder and Herder, 1962) pp. 79-80.

Chapter Five

UNITY: EVERYWHERE BUT NOWHERE

THE TWENTIENTH CENTURY IS THE ECUMENICAL ERA. TALK
of unity is heard on all hands. Newspapers give more publicity to Christian reunion than to other religious topics. On
the top level most of the Christian churches of the world are
meeting, negotiating, consulting, and working. Unity is everywhere.

If unity exists as an idea and ideal, as a reality in the
plan of God which is striven for in the work of men, it
exists wherever the Church is represented. Yet when one
wishes to locate the ecumenical impulse in Christian people
he has difficulty finding its place. In local situations, where
most Christians expend most of their spiritual energy and
where they have greatest opportunity for God's service, unity
is least apparent.

To speak of gains in the public sphere is certainly to
point to something worthwhile. To say that on the level
of the "power elites" Christians are meeting with each other
is again to point to a great gain. To give publicity to these
encounters is to serve the Christian cause. In this chapter,
as we examine the question of "local unity," it is important
not to undervalue the unity that is everywhere but hard to
isolate on the local scene.

In no age has it been more important to be able to point
to gains in the public sphere than in our own. For the world

that we know and shall continue to know is marked by the crisscrossing of values and influences. Mass media of communication bring remote ideas near. Population growth pushes people of different value-systems nearer each other. Mobility causes people to be uprooted and to face new patterns of living. In the age of the advertiser people have learned to think in "images."

In such a time the public "image" of the churches is important. The life of Roman Catholicism as a whole, or of Methodism as a whole, suffers when a part of it is demonstrably working contrary to Christian patterns. The life of each is improved and its work simplified if the public brings the proper expectation to it, based upon the proper projection of "images." The picture of divided churches engaged in holy wars long belonged and to some extent still belongs in the public mind. Wherever this image is vivid, people are less likely to explore Christian claims than where one Christ is adored and offered to men.

On the level of these public realities each gain means protection for people. The holy wars of past centuries were occasioned by the leaders of various religious groups when they misread or threatened the purpose of others. The nineteenth-century Protestant-Catholic conflicts in America, for instance, were intensified because people misunderstood each other, because leaders were not in contact with each other across religious lines. Convents were burned; ugly tracts were printed; anti-Catholic societies were formed and anti-Protestant attitudes were developed because of failure to communicate. Catholics in their ghettoes and Protestants in their sectors and villages and valleys were not guided by their leadership to understand and trust each other. Indeed, leadership was responsible for exaggerating difference.

The public image of large religious units organizing to wage war on each other has changed. The daily press brings new and surprising accounts of irenic Roman Catholic spokesmen.   What was not dreamed of six years ago is no longer a cause for wonder, as Catholicism on its world-wide level sets its house in order and seeks better relations with Protestantism and Orthodoxy. The acceptance of Russian and other Iron Curtain churches into the ecumenical organizations is well known to be one of the few instances of real contact between East and West. The co-operation of Orthodox and Protestant groups in the World Council of Churches should remove motivation and passion from the older intra-Protestant struggles.

The real gains of "unity everywhere" are portrayed, however, not in the pronouncements and meetings of organizations or the development of joint statements on issues. It is when the Church acts, when the churches work in concert, that these gains are most apparent. To take an instance: during 1963 one could pick up the newpapers almost any day and see stories concerning the activities of clergymen and leaders of Protestant groups taking part, however tacitly, in demonstrations which would better the racial situation. Such activities and news events wear no denominational stamp. No governmental department in a nation which is pluralistic would think of consulting only one of the churches on a policy which concerns all. Can one imagine an art gallery which wants to have an exhibit on "Religious Art" and asks the participants about their denominational affiliation? A publisher who wishes to gather the finest Christian thinkers on any particular topic would impoverish his symposium by limiting the spokesmen to one denominational group. Conferences on church-state relations, on theology, and on Christian action are now ecumenical in their make-up almost as a matter of instinct.

These interactions of the churches' power elites, we have said, are of no little consequence on the Christian scene. The imagination of the public is shaped by reports of them. Insofar as a secular world extends any kind of curiosity at all to religious affairs, it will extend it to activities which are intrinsically interesting and not to those which advertise themselves because they belong to one church among the churches.

Unity is everywhere. But this is not the case locally. In how many local communities have visible signs appeared which would suggest that Protestantism and Catholicism are in conversation? Popes John XXIII and Paul VI and a whole covey of cardinals may address Protestants as "separated brothers" and Protestant leaders may return the address. But on the local level old animosities remain, almost as if no signals from the larger Christian body are telegraphed to the local realities where people meet each other daily.

The local scene of parish and congregation is the most retarded as far as ecumenical progress is concerned. Perhaps in its apathy or bewilderment in this field it is merely providing another evidence to critical social thinkers that it has served its purposes and outlived its usefulness as an organizing center for Christian life. The parish, so captive of local prejudice and so often so much the product of class instincts and personal pride, may not soon be able to become an instrument for good. This is the argument of many of the most learned and concerned social thinkers today. Hans Hoekendijk in Holland, Gibson Winter and Peter Berger in the United States, Max Thurian and Roger Schutz in France, the leaders of the lay academies in Germany and the house churches in England, are either saying explicitly or acting implicitly on the assumption that new forms of corporate life will have to appear. Only when the local congregation is no longer the focus of Christian work will there be new vitality of thought, worship, and service.

As impressive as such argument is and as hopeful as we may be for the emergence of "new forms," it would be irresponsible to abandon all concern for existing forms. The parishes now serve to gather most of the energies of Christian people. Out of them come the new ministers and leaders. There quiet works of love in Christ's name continue. The sacramental life of the Church goes on there. People preach and are listened to and sometimes heard. In the local congregations there are daily evidence of real generosity and imagination. In them are great numbers of people who are penalized by circumstances they cannot control, so that they cannot show forth the Christian unity they profess and desire.

Somehow the local scene deserves attention. Persons finally have to be identified with some local settings; sociological views of the Church which abstract themselves from such prosaic and workaday situations do not do justice to life as lived or the Church as chartered. Persons come together. They will not always be located at the universities or lay academies; they will seldom have access to the mass media; they will usually be "officially unimportant people." They must be given opportunities of overcoming divisions — opportunities that they have not yet possessed.

In recent years the World Council of Churches has developed and agreed upon a first formal definition of such local implications of unity. We shall quote it, emphasizing the crucial phrase and letting it stand as the measurement for what follows:

> We believe that the unity which is both God's will and His gift to His Church is being made visible as *all in each place who are baptized into Jesus Christ* and confess Him as Lord and Saviour are brought by the Holy Spirit into *one fully committed fellowship,* holding the one apostolic faith, preaching the one Gospel, breaking the one bread, joining in common prayer, and having a corporate life reaching out in witness and service to all and who at the same time are united with the whole Christian fellowship in all places and all ages in such wise that ministry and members are accepted by all, and that all can act and speak together as occasion requires for the tasks to which God calls His people.

This is a magnificent statement, apparently incontrovertible in the light of the New Testament's picture of the Church.

But who pays attention to the New Testament's picture? Cite such a theological statement concerning local unity and immediately a host of defenses appear. "That is pure idealism." "That is too farfetched and visionary." "Are you dreamers?" "You have to be conscious of history and of the circumstances of church life." "I believe in one, holy, catholic, apostolic Church — but you'll never get *me* to recognize the Baptists." We must agree: the statement seems to be idealism; it is farfetched in the range of today's parochial prose. It does call the Church back to its original charter and away from some of the vagaries of historical development. It does call for surprising crossing of historical organizational lines. The "fully committed fellowship" of "all in each place who are baptized in Jesus Christ" seems so far removed from the context of possibilities today that it seems idle to discuss.

Did the churches make a mistake by agreeing on this statement? It is hard to find someone who will say that it is unjust to the biblical picture of the Church or unsatisfying to the minds of those who seek Christian solidarity. It simply commits people to the impossible. Is not the making of such an assertion merely one more way of drawing public attention to the failure of the Church? Would it not be better to learn to swim before one begins to dive? Why advertise the distance between what we are and what we must become? Why not be silent and let the outsider make his attacks while we divert his attention to the Church's strong points?

All of these questions have a logical weight but a theological invalidity. After a half-century of working toward unity it was logical that great numbers of people would begin to ask: Toward what does this point? What is the outline of the fulfillment? When the Christian leadership began to try to answer this question they found the logic of the New Testament and the Christian tradition pressing them to the kind of statement that was produced. As a matter of fact, the definition was left vague and general so that it could be a minimum and would not limit Christian work toward re-union. It was conceived that the Christian mission would best advance under such local circumstances, though of course it was not assumed that the mission would have to await the arrival of such circumstances!

In the previous chapter we tried to outline four interrelated forms of collective Christian life. Now one can test them in the local setting. At the center was the ecumenical conscious-ness. In this consciousness the Christian sees one fact through and beyond all division, that if the Spirit of Christ is formed in another I am already one with him in the new creation. My positive relation to him is now more important than are relations built with others through the accident of "belonging" to the same denomination.

Does this consciousness operate in the local community where there are numbers of churches? Certainly, valiant efforts are made by certain ministers and lay elites. Common programs, comity in placing of churches, the expression of a Christian spirit — these flow from the efforts of such people. Again we may surmise that for the more casual church members a nebulous back-of-the-mind idea couched in phrases such as "the invisible Church" gives some sort of believability to the Apostles' Creed's profession of belief in the Church. At the fringes are numbers of nominal Chris-tians who have solved the ecumenical problem in their own way: the differences between Christians have no validity be-cause the quest for truth has no importance.

What the local situation ordinarily lacks, however, is the carefully planned and sustained daily ministry to the ecu-menical spirit. What divides has been institutionalized and is regularly fed and nourished. What unites seems remote, abstract, ideal, and is neglected. It does not catch the im-agination; "the ecumenical movement has not caught on."

We referred to the second kind of grasp on corporate

Christian life as "confessional." By this we meant the person's and the congregation's act of appropriating the tradition of the Church as it has come to them, making it their own, and saying, This we believe! Where the ecumenical spirit does not find an outlet, the confessional expression is without doubt the most fruitful alternative. The dedicated and informed laity whose faith has sought understanding will inevitably speak "confessionally." Since the confessions of the branches of Christianity strive to remain integrally related to the center and root of the faith, one should be cheered by confessional awareness.

Unfortunately, in the competitive situation, the confessions are not permitted to serve as uniting agents. Instead the superiority of one over the other is advertised. Since most elements of the faith are similar in the main confessions, it becomes necessary to gain advantage by magnifying differences. While ecumenical Christianity devotes a decade to careful biblical study of baptism, it remains necessary in the local community for Baptists to advertise their unique views on baptism and for others to condemn the Baptists and to advertise the superiority of their own hold on biblical truth. While ecumenical Christianity makes careful historical study of orders and church government, it remains necessary in the local community for the Episcopalians to emphasize the virtues of retaining bishops in apostolic succession and for their competitors to advertise the democratic values of congregational polity.

Since the differences between confessions are so slight on so many points, it becomes necessary for a caste of professionals to develop who can cope with these subtleties. The result is that the ordained minister usually becomes the custodian of these fine points. The layman is carefully instructed to learn that there are such issues and that they are somehow important. He pays a professional to serve as guardian and propagandist, and so takes leave of the responsibility to concern *himself* with the Christian tradition. The liabilities, not the assets of confessionalism, are seen in the competitive local community. Theological seriousness becomes self-defeating.

Tradition, or better, the grasp of traditions was seen to be the third element which holds together Christian people. These are certainly much more vivid in the local community. The townspeople know these traditions. They know which church is clique-dominated and which is friendly. They know which one favors Gothic architecture and which favors Georgian. One, they know, sings classic and dull Christian hymns, while in another it is traditional to sing gospel songs. One can be counted on each year for a strawberry festival, and another traditionally raffles off a Cadillac. One has the tradition of educating children profoundly; another has a Sunday school as a mere cultural rounding out of the parish. In one the minister chants and wears historic vestments. In another he shouts and wears a black gown. All these traditional elements which, it must be noted, are far removed from central Christian concerns do provide citizens with issues. Everyone can be an expert on matters of taste and appearances. Violent prejudices grow out of these; authentic Christian nurture can in part depend upon them. As necessary, as inevitable as these traditions are, in divided Christianity they are exaggerated. In the local situation they become the most visible wares on the cafeteria line as people come to "the church of their choice." Inevitably, attachment to these traditions of local origin detracts from more nearly central Christian concerns.

In the fourth kind of collective form the greatest offense lies. This is in denominationalism, which we defined as attachment to the organizational accidents which perpetuate traditions and serve to embody the confessions. Denominationalism is, of course, no problem in one-church communities. But wherever the local community is confronted

with great numbers of options in religion, the claims of denominationalism will be advanced most openly. The denomination is given over to exaggerating and perpetuating
Christian differences — at least until a denominational merger
points to the irrelevance of past differences between two
groups and subtracts, by one, from the offense of division.

In a pluralist or competitive society one cannot escape some
form of denominationalism. Each attempt to be non-denominational, both in history and in contemporary local communities, has only led in fact to the founding of one more
denomination. As with nationalism in the modern world,
one must say: you can change your sect but not your religion.
The denomination must work for its survival. This forces
each congregation to bear its good name in the local community. Each is expected to act in such a way so as not to
embarrass the larger denominational operation. It is expected that the local congregation will "produce a good
return" on the church body's investments or will organize its
affairs to help support the body's goals uncritically. While
ostensibly the denomination is, in secular terms, a product of
the consensus of the congregations, it tends to take on an
independent power of its own. It becomes the apparatus
which constantly reproduces new generations of denominationalists to keep the ecumenical spirit from being con-
solidated. It is the welter of denominations and not the
small family of confessions or the variety of harmless traditions
which most causes impatience with Christianity and which
elicits the superficial question which makes a profound one:
"Why don't the churches get together?"

The preceding is made up of a mass of generalizations;
most readers can document them by thinking how churches
actually operate in their own local communities. To make the
claims more concrete, however, we shall illustrate by reference
to a typical local community. What was discovered there is

parallel to the findings of every other community that, to our knowledge, has come under sociological scrutiny. The community in question is "Springdale," a traditional community in upstate New York.[1] While it may be argued that Springdale represents a passing kind of setting in an urbanizing world, one may agree and then note that the sociological studies of emerging urban communities and suburbs point to an exaggeration of these tendencies.

Chapter 9 of Vidich and Bensman, called "Religion and the Affirmation of the Present," deals with the place of the church (pp. 227ff.). "Church-going is of major importance in the social life of Springdale simply because it constitutes so great a part of the publicly visible community activity. Church activities involve relatively large groups of people and occur in conspicuous places at fixed times." Four Protestant churches, Baptist, Episcopal, Congregational, and Methodist predominate. Seven other small churches are represented nearby. Church activities represent fifty percent of all organized social activities. "The pattern of activities of any one church is relatively indistinguishable from any other." All sub-organizations support their own social programs, "a fact which again multiplies the number of church-connected activities. These include the church supper, the ice-cream social, the bake sale, the rummage sale, the men's supper, the hay rides, the picnics; there are missionary societies, Bible classes, etc. in the Baptist church which rejects the money-making programs of the others. Churches co-operate in planning a social calendar because the same clientele supports the public events of all. They are divided only for worship, education, mission."

Typically, the churches are made up of professional people; "only a small percentage of industrial workers, who are

---

[1] Arthur J. Vidich and Joseph Bensman, *Small Town in Mass Society* (Princeton: Princeton University Press, 1958).

otherwise similar to the professionals in style of living, are church-involved." New migrants join on the basis of prior disposition and local tradition but not on the basis of the actual theology of the local churches.

The minister "mediates between the local church and the religious life of the outside world." He has an experience of personal ties outside the community which he has garnered in seminary and denominational life. His people lack this and consider him an impermanent resident because of these connections. Whatever may be in his mind concerning the ecumenical church is not easily communicated to theirs. "To a large extent he is unable to express what he personally believes, except for accepted, uncontroversial dogma." The world-oriented pronouncements of the denominations are themselves not promulgated locally because of local prejudice.

> What is interesting . . . in connection with the policies of national church organizations, is that ecumenicalism, the great contemporary movement to unify the Protestant churches, receives practically no *public* expression in Springdale.

The upper echelons of denominations "have been overwhelmingly concerned" with ecumenical organization. Periodicals are full of these concerns. "It would be quite unthinkable for any minister in Springdale to direct public attention to even . . . a diluted statement" of the ecumenical bodies when they express themselves in world-oriented terms. Criticism is directed to "intellectual" ministers: "He's a brilliant man, but what this church needs is a good organizer."

What about local-level ecumenicalism? Vidich and Bensman find several evidences. There are joint religious services on two or three occasions a year; summer Bible classes, when attendance is weak, are held in common; there may be a community choir for secular events. Churches jointly sponsor a "Go to Church Week," an American Legion "Back to God" movement. There is a ministerial council. "Ecumenicalism is in conflict with the essentially expansive and missionary nature of each individual church."

Church unity and church mission are seen to be in conflict. There is conflict over "allocation of shares" of the market for congregational membership. When church activities are merged in co-operative programs the members' attention may be drawn from their own denomination and local church. "The loss of exclusive domain over members" is a problem for the minister "because his work is judged by his superiors largely in terms of the size and vigor of his congregation. . . . Hence, in the midst of ecumenicalism, the various churches act to preserve their differences.

> This is done by publicly cooperating in interchurch activities while privately disparaging each other's ministers and churches. . . . Mutual criticisms and attacks are made on ministers, theology, organizational structure — on almost anything — but are always expressed privately among the ingroup and, hence, serve the purpose of minimizing the impact of publicly practiced ecumenicalism.

At another level the interest in preserving congregational difference leads to a special form of "local *sub-rosa* ecumenicalism" which permits external cordiality and internal preservation of differences.

Thus ecumenical practice is ritualized, so that no church gains psychological advantage. Joint services are carefully guarded events. Congregations come and sit in a body apart from other congregations, so they do not really meet. "To a large extent ecumenical practice brings people together in a physical sense only." There are "tacit anti-poaching agreements" which have the effect but not the sanctions of law. Listen to the missionary implication:

> A minister limits his pastoral work to his own congregation. More than this, the fear of being accused of proselytizing, of competing for souls, is so great that a minister has practically nothing but formal social contacts outside the membership of his own congregation.

"Nonetheless, pseudo-ecumenicalism forces the minister to employ other means of competition for membership." Thus there are often minor violations of agreements, "creative misinterpretations of agreements" and other forms of competition. *"The bulk of the population which is not church-going is not the object of missionary work."* Missionary work is geared to newcomers and to those already churched. It is inefficient to try to interest the unchurched; or often, the local unchurched are simply ignored — a feat which would seem difficult in a community of 1700 adults.

> While the mission opportunity on the local scene goes unseen, each church carries on an extensive missionary program for non-Christians in remote places. The community of the damned still exists, but it is not noticed in one's immediate environment.

The authors continue by pointing out that problems raised by ecumenicalism are solved by differences in theology. But these differences could hardly be characterized by our term "confessionalism." "Theology, *as used* [emphasis ours], emphasizes the differences and helps to preserve the jurisdictional boundaries between the churches. On the theological grounds no minister completely commits himself to ecumenicalism, keeping, as it were, a theological ace in the hole to prevent the ecumenical absorption of his own church." Each finds some reason for separation. "For the minister they represent sales points that competitors cannot meet." All ministers emphasize only distinguishing doctrine and highlight them as church-membership badges. "Theology itself, then, becomes an organizational device for holding and recruiting members and, as such, it becomes a branch of administration."

The Baptists of Springdale represented a partial departure from the general practice. They were often neither overtly ecumenical, nor were they so in a *sub-rosa* sense. They were a conservative group that was merely non- or anti-ecumenical.

Gibson Winter has discovered attitudes comparable to all

of the foregoing in the localism of suburban churches; Victor Obenhaus finds similar theological unconcern coupled with profession of interest in denominational differences in rural areas; Gerhard Lenski has found overlays of the same in the city. Students of "foreign mission" fields regularly find similar evidence.

The ecumenical center does not often reveal itself except in routinized forms; the confessional consciousness is transformed into "theology for competition"; traditions give local color for advertised differences; even the best elements of denominationalism on its inter-regional levels are not filtered to the local. It may be argued that the World Council of Churches' hope that "all in each place become one" brings with it some problems of its own. Will people carry on missionary work without denominational competition as a goad? Will people take theology seriously when they are in a "fully committed fellowship" of oneness? Theologically speaking, these are not valid questions. The Christian tradition commits us to the view that the one Church must find more unified expression. But even on purely practical terms one may argue: we could not possibly do worse than we are now doing in reaching the unchurched of the communities or in promoting theological seriousness. Perhaps for a century or so something else might be tried experimentally!

Is it useful to speak of a quest for a "fully committed fellowship" among all confessors of the name of Christ so long as no substantial historic differences between Protestants and Catholics are overcome? These differences are at present apparently insoluble. No one can wait for their organizational resolution before he undertakes a new mission. Yet one must answer: it *is* useful as it is necessary to direct ecumenical strivings so concretely. The definition is narrow enough to form a focus, broad enough to allow for surprise. Presently, were progress to be made in solving the most profound kinds of differences — such as those between Protestants and

Catholics — on the "upper echelon," the local churches would be untrained to adapt to the bettered situation and would probably resist.

A rather hopeless picture has been painted. From the instance of a local region and by reference to others it is suggested that a baptized person has little to look forward to. He cannot remain in isolation and experience Christian fullness. He must somehow relate himself to corporate Chrisianity. In the local setting that usually means some sort of residential parish. But his theology and his practice come into immediate conflict. By "uniting" with a unit he increases his division from the larger Body. Are there not mitigating circumstances, and are there not compensations or even defenses for the present situation?

The picture described at full length was drawn from the kind of pluralistic environment experienced most vividly in the United States. The division of Christianity on the local level is experienced not at all where all Christians go to the same church, and is not so dramatic where only two or three churches are present. In Augsburg, Germany, there is a medieval church building divided down the center. From one side Catholics enter for their worship; through doors at the other end the Evangelicals come to their church. To local residents it must often seem as if from eternity some were destined to enter from one door and from eternity others were expected to find the other door. There is little prospect of reunion and little offense in separation. In European bookstalls one can buy popular magazines inside whose cover, in each issue, is an article on religion "by a representative of one of the two branches of Christianity," meaning Catholicism and Evangelicalism. Viewed as two peaks and at such close range there is little offense. We have been describing the exaggerated circumstances where so many church bodies are active in a local community. Perhaps matters are better elsewhere. Still, the major missionary efforts of the churches have been occurring in these areas of competition and they will remain the prime problem areas.

Another contributor to partial relief in the disease of localism is the role of mass media. In Springdale little of what happened ecumenically was presented because ministers found it unprofitable or unwise to do so. This situation is changing. The public side of the ecumenical movement has grown so that, while its local meaning is not made clear, the larger reality does begin to become part of consciousness. The personality of Pope John XXIIII, the existence of the Vatican Council, the acceptance of Russian churchmen into the World Council of Churches, and the controversial pronouncements of ecumenical bodies have kept them in the public eye. Sooner or later, we must presume, there will be a ground swell of local acceptance. Perhaps the followers will one day advance beyond the leaders; "Why don't the churches get together?" could become the question of the dedicated Christians; "the people don't want ecumenicity" could be less true — and the mass media of the secular world would have to be thanked.

These portraits and prospects are small hopes compared to the problems of local communities, and the "all in each place" motif deservedly must remain a daily judgment on all churches. It will encounter formidable opposition on several grounds.

First is the practical. There is a certain kind of "get the job done" mentality which is held in high acclaim and for which something should be said. When a counselor reaches a certain point in the discussion of love he must suddenly turn on a troubled couple and say: "Now, don't be so conscious of every move you make. Don't analyze every motive. Just start loving; act your love, show it." In the church something should be said for the "doers" who do not just talk about mission but who do something. Without question, they are a judgment upon the dilettante versions of ecumenicity which are "all talk and not action" and whose participants use their academic status as an excuse not to get their hands dirty in the church. There are good reasons to admire those who grow impatient with talk of progress and set out to work with unfortunate circumstances. The anti-ecumenical groups which work on the marginal elements of the community are not bothered by concerns for Christian unity; they just "do their job." Groups which are unconcerned with comity in placing churches or who violate agreements can later justify their actions by producing numbers of people in a congregation. One must carefully measure these realities.

Another line of defense and one which is approached just as frequently can be called "the democratic plea." This amounts to a resistance to ecumenicity because reunion of churches could lead to large combines and totalitarian organizations. It is assumed that competitive Christianity will automatically produce small units where the individual will have more right to assert himself and to control church life. Thus a Methodist bishop can criticize merger movements which include and thus unsettle his institutions. He can say that such merger would lead to a "super church." In this familiar argument the mere fact of the size of a body militates against Christian freedom. The same Methodist bishop, however, works industriously for the enlargement of Methodism with no concern for what its growth will do to the person.

In a different context one could enlarge upon the tired institutionalism of the ecumenical organizations. They must be brought under critical observation constantly. But one charge against them, that they are encroaching bureaucracies, is hard to substantiate. The annual budget of the world headquarters of the World Council of Churches in Geneva is hardly larger than that of countless individual congregations in member churches within it. The staff of full-time employees is smaller than the staff of many of the hundreds of thousands of congregations which make it up.

The size of the unit should make little difference. Size

is relative. The growth of congregations and denominations, like the growth of the population as a whole, brings the necessity for adjustment to the problems of each successive size. If a Roman Catholic parishioner lacks "freedom," this is not because of the size of world Catholicism but because of other factors. It is easier to be free from the discipline of many a large denomination than in many a small one; it is also often easier to gain a hearing in a larger one. The old arguments for or against reunion movements because they would "give more weight and power" to a cluster of churches (like the Protestants) against others (like the Catholics) or against other forces (like atheists) are disappearing and should disappear. They bring up problems which are not directly related to the ecumenical movement but are implied in the power and pride of all forms of collective life in the world.

For the ecumenical movement the question should not be: How do we preserve man's autonomy and individualism by keeping the units small? Rather, it should read: What should be the character and quality of our collective life — the only kind of Christian life we know — so that full Christian personhood can emerge?

Still another line of defense for the current forms of localism can be implied under the term "loyalty." It is often argued that one is unrealistic if he expects that loyalties can be summoned around abstract ideals, remote realities, broadly based hopes. Whoever has attended a rally of the Knights of Columbus or a meeting of a Protestant denomination's laymen's group; whoever has heard them sing the songs and parade the banners, repeat the vows and rally the laggards, resort to family jokes and local-color humor will understand the power of loyalty in a smaller, more definable group. What is this one, holy, catholic, apostolic Church in contrast to such vivid local realities? Will not much of the genuine devotion and real energy depart from Christian groups if they are deprived of group-centered loyalties which bring them into contact with their own kind? This is a formidable argument and cannot lightly be dismissed. Still, many questions can be asked. Who places such a high value on "loyalty"? Has the concept been examined psychologically? Is the loyalty devoted to specifically Christian goals; can it not also be directed to goals which directly controvert Christianity? Is not much of the banner-waving mere pride and selfishness?

Some positive assertions are also in order. The hymnals are full of hymns which stir men's souls and yet are devoted singularly to the whole Christian mission and the Church as such. The hymns of the missionary era were not written for particular benevolent societies or denominations: they were written to advance the whole cause. Have we lacked the imagination to develop a symbolism for the ecumenical age because the energies of Christians have been drained on trivial denominational goals? There are more serious questions to raise.

To my mind the most valid missionary question to ask is this: Would a local unity not further remove the churches from the unreached in society? The studies by such as Vidich and Bensman reveal that the denominations most predisposed to ecumenicity are the "main-stream groups" which are most inclined to be made up of the middle classes, the professionals, the respectable in a community. The uncooperative groups were more ready to deal with "marginal" people. Would ecumenicity mean cultural blandness? Would it attract the safe people? Certainly, if Christian reunion occurs to exclude large groups of people it can hardly be an instrument for Christian service.

Once again, the first question to be asked of the charge that the marginal people would be forgotten is this: Are we so sure that the current definitions of "marginal" are permanent? A welfare society is constantly causing economic changes which jostle existing classes in most societies. Universal education as a possibility will cause redefinition of marginality. Is not much of the "fringe-group" growth among marginal people one which still serves to bypass great numbers of others, such as intellectuals or the main group of laborers? What about the secularized people who have not yet been reached by the churches and are less likely to be reached by them if they are directing their efforts toward "religious" types in the middle classes and the "margins"? More positively, one can assert that the attempt to bring a "fully committed fellowship" to reality in each place need not be done at the expense of cultural variety but only at the expense of selfish competition. Let the current mission of anti-ecumenical groups serve as a reminder of the need for the "mission to the marginal" in the uniting churches.

Before leaving this topic I feel constrained to mention several matters which might detract somewhat from a grow-ing romanticism associated with the statistics of growth in anti-ecumenical bodies. They have several "things going for them." They can stress one particular dogma with such verve and clarity that people left behind by the consensus of Chris-tians in the main stream of society will rally around it at the expense of the catholic fullness of faith. The non-co-operative group can also "pick its spots," watching for the areas where people predisposed to its theology reside. They need carry little responsibility to the whole range of residence. Some of their growth is merely a subtraction from the potential of others and not the rescue from the world of someone who certainly would not be reached otherwise. Finally, as pointed out earlier in the book, missions in the Christian Church can-not be defined merely as snatching one more soul into sal-vation without regard for all that Christ's servants should do in the world. The anti-ecumenical group, we observed, trades on the capital of the co-operative groups and squanders some of the time the churches must borrow to learn how to cope with a secular world.

Now it is time to set the cards on the table. What has been wrong with the argument of this chapter has been that it has been based chiefly on sociological calculation, on the vagaries of human personality and current class structures in a competitive society. Actually, only one question should sting Christians: "Is Christ divided?" Is Christ's prayer "that they may all be one *so that* the world may believe" frustrated by our practices? The final word on divisive practices is almost the first word (I Cor. 1:12-13): "What I mean is that each one of you says, 'I belong to Paul,' or 'I belong to Apollos,' or 'I belong to Cephas,' or 'I belong to Christ.' Is Christ divided? Was Paul crucified for you?" The practical unfolding of church life in the future will belong to people awakened by this question to seek new forms. "Who is sufficient for these things? For we are not, like so many, *peddlers of God's word*; but as men of sincerity, as commissioned by God, in the sight of God we speak in Christ" (II Cor. 2:17).

Roland Allen once wrote a book *The Spontaneous Expansion of the Church and the Causes Which Hinder It.* A sort of "National Association of Manufacturers" mentality which justifies Christian competition on secular grounds of efficiency and practicality should elicit a book *The Spontaneous Reunion of the Church and the Causes Which Hinder It.* Allen knew that the Church does not expand simply, without the responding efforts of men whose self-centeredness must be overcome by the Spirit of Christ. So, too, reunion is not spontaneous. Men must work to show forth the unity which it is God's alone to give. But dare Christians be content with arguments from historical accident and practical necessity when the mandates which charter the Church are clear?

The situation is "desperate but not serious": desperate because, unchecked, it can spell the end of seriousness in the life of the one Church; not serious, because men can work the works of God even while the local situations do not provide full opportunities to show forth Christ's one Body. Two-thirds of the world is not confronted by Jesus Christ. Perhaps the majority of this population is not committed to any religion. The men of the secular environment surrounding Christianity "round out their lives" without openness to His claim on them. In such a world, catering to the prejudices of the good burghers of Springdale with a denominational cafeteria provides little basis for serious Christian effort anywhere.

Where are the models for the "fully committed fellowship" in each place? There are none, in a way. For a fully committed fellowship is in some senses an "eschatological reality." Where men are sinful the perfection of Christian fellowship will not be revealed. The attempts to express such fellowship will be accomplished by new and surprising forms of resistance. Still, in the mergers such as we have seen in South India and Canada, in the trans-confessional conversations in the United States, in the occasional exceptions where real Christian unity is shown in local communities, there are models and inspirations. There is no need to impoverish the final form by precommitting Christians to too precise a model. The World Council statement calls upon unity with the Christian tradition "in all places and all ages" — surely this catalog should offer some options more attractive than those we possess, some skeletons that can invite inquiry even if they cannot be clothed with flesh today.

Sometimes the local emphasis on better relations between Christians fails to capture the imagination because it is assumed that fulfillment will merely involve people in more trivial detail. If I do not care about the dartball team at my church or the fish fry at the Methodists', the salary of the Baptist minister or the constitution of the Lutheran Church, won't I be drawn into such marginal concerns in a "fully committed fellowship" of confessors? The way the question is put marks it as dated by the era in which it was born, an age marked by trivialization in church life because Christians' real goals have been lost. One must repose his hope and his confidence in the knowledge that a re-formed Church would be purged of the nagging triviality brought about by competition. A more profound fellowship, learning, and service can be called forth whenever men answer and care about their answer to the question: "Is Christ divided?"

Chapter Six

A COMPLICATION WHICH SIMPLIFIES

A GRAPH REPRESENTING THE CHRISTIAN POPULATION OF THE world reveals one factor which limited all talk of unity in the first half-century after Edinburgh. Slightly more than half the "pie" of the graph was in no way involved directly in the ecumenical movement. The *Weltkirchen Lexikon* of 1960 presents such a graph in which 50.71% of the Christians are of one communion and under one obedience. This half of the Christian membership in today's world, the Roman Catholic half, stood aloof and seemed remote. The men of vision of 1910 seldom considered the Church of Rome in their plans or hopes.

Roman Catholicism was just emerging from a self-defensive century. It was preoccupied, as was Protestantism, with establishing missions. It was bewildered in the face of the secular attacks of the century. Its stronghold in Western Europe was undergoing political change which threatened Catholic hegemony. The popes, notably Pius IX, had re-acted violently, attacking almost everything beyond the Catholic wall as a threat to faith. Invitations to a church of such a heritage were seldom sent and, when sent, seldom acted upon. It was too busy with its own fence-mending and wall-building. Many Protestants in the ecumenical movement were anti-Catholic. In some instances Protestant reunion even revealed a subtly anti-Roman bias. "If we get together we

19884

can present to the world a united voice which can counter that of Rome." While such sentiment was seldom overt and seldom occurred on the more responsible levels, no doubt much popular support for Protestant ecumenicity was oriented against Rome.

While this situation prevailed, there was a partiality and hollowness to the ecumenical endeavor. What kind of Christian solidarity would be revealed to the world if Christians merely formed two or three large blocs of competition and mistrust? Would such unity be *Christian*?

Through the fifty years since 1910 we have seen a progressive broadening of the scope of hope for reunion. Originally it incorporated what we have called "main-stream Protestantism." By this we mean representatives of the conservative Reformation: Anglicanism, Lutheranism, the Reformed communions. To this we add those heirs of the "left wing of the Reformation" which, through the years, had drifted toward the center. Here we would include groups such as the Baptists. The fundamentalists and conservative evangelicals, though oriented toward missions, did not feel at home in the earlier stages of the movement because of theological differences. The "Pentecostal" edge of Protestantism was disturbed by the churchly assumptions of ecumenicity.

Through the years there has been a constant broadening of Protestant participation. But the coziness of the evangelical house was destroyed by the gradual introduction of Eastern Orthodoxy. Eastern Orthodoxy represented "the stranger" but, since he was willing to come in, he was welcomed. The presence of Orthodoxy has represented tremendous complication to those who seek to produce documents which portray the consensus of Christianity. Orthodoxy is intransigent in its view that it alone represents the pure and true Christian tradition. It does not regard the other churches as being churches in the full sense of the term. It is hesitant to grant "churchly" status to the councils of churches. Yet

Orthodoxy was *spatially* separated from Protestantism. The two portions of the non-Roman half of the Christian "pie" supplemented each other geographically. Where Eastern Christians were strong, Protestants were thinly represented. Since Protestantism is a movement in Western Christianity, its domains seldom saw many Orthodox. Protestantism was aggressively missionary in the nineteenth century, but Orthodoxy was not. The two could be friendly because they remembered little of each other, expected little of each other, and were surprised at every *entente,* every agreement, every friendly gesture.

From main-stream Protestantism to inclusive Protestantism to Protestant-Orthodox conversation is still a long way from the great complication introduced after fifty years. With surprising suddenness after 1959 "ecumenical" has come to mean something other than a Protestant family reunion on Western soil. Now ecumenism, *both as spirit and as movement,* includes Roman Catholicism. Insofar as public interest in ecumenicity can be aroused at all, it is being awakened to this newer reality. Insofar as the world outside the Church is concerned, this is the only form which surprises and holds suspense. Insofar as radical Protestantism and conservative Catholicism are concerned, this is the phase of the movement which threatens and must be fought off. Insofar as "main-stream ecumenism" of a half-century is concerned, this is the perplexing complication. One cannot theologically deny the value of Roman and non-Roman relations. One cannot sociologically or psychologically see ways in which this involvement will come to fruition. This chapter will concern itself with reflection on the meaning of Roman Catholicism's presence and with one positive lesson learned from Catholicism's existing form.

Throughout these chapters we have implied an expanding circle. It goes something like this: Christians possess now enough unity and ecumenical spirit to renew their mission to the world. Without such renewal ecumenism is meaningless and its movement is tired and self-centered. Meanwhile, renewed mission will further the movement to unity, will give new energy to the tired, new youth to a prematurely aged movement, new openness to what was becoming self-concerned. Unity produces mission produces unity produces mission, etc. That is the circle. Is it not decisively shattered when Catholicism enters the scene? For certainly it is foolish to talk in the context of today's possibilities of "merger" between Protestants and Catholics. How can mission wait for such merger? Will not concern for such *entente* paralyze mission?

Admittedly, it is more feasible to think of Catholic participation in the conciliar forms of the unity movement. As a matter of fact Rome is already there represented unofficially in countless ways and officially in many other carefully defined ways. Indeed, many Roman Catholics are beginning to say that there are no real doctrinal reasons for them to be aloof. There would be no complication or contradiction to the Catholic doctrine of the Church were Rome to be incorporated into existing world-wide councils of Christian conversation. But will not increasing Roman Catholic involvement further muffle the clarity of the movement? Can any "joint documents" between churches of the Roman obedience and those which reject the papacy really speak in other than general terms? If Eastern Othodoxy has been a complicating voice, what about Rome?

These questions concerning the remote possibility of concrete Roman involvement serve to portray how hopeless it is to peg Christian mission to this organizational relation. At the same time, it is difficult to see how biblically-oriented people can permanently disregard the one-half of those who call Jesus Christ Lord, who worship the divine Trinity, who also say "Our Father," *who want to be regarded as brothers* but who disagree on many fundamentals of faith and who are of the Roman obedience.

If Rome is to be thought of, the ecumenical spirit dare not be confined to existing forms of the ecumenical movement. The movement may point toward Christian union whereas we may have to learn to speak of unity; or it may hope for unity whereas with Rome one may have to hope only for solidarity. Maybe solidarity is too much: maybe concord in the negative sense, meaning only the cessation of hostility and the lessening of conflict, may be all that can be sought. What should be the organizational hopes in such a time?

One who works himself up to this point and who honestly wants to face all that is involved here is tempted to despair. How much easier it would have been if only Protestants had pretended that they alone were the Church and had proceeded from there to set their own house in order! Would it not have been better to create the impression that Christ's brothers were only those who, after 1517, rejected Rome? But evangelical Christians were unready to "cut the pie in two" and throw away one half. They were unready to tailor their doctrine of the Church to meet the conveniences of sociology and the prejudices of half-Christians. They are now "stuck" with a doctrine of the Church which complicates practice. Enemies of the ecumenical spirit can take delight in this travail. They can hope that the burden of the ecumenical vision and the apparent impossibility of carrying it out will weary the dreamers and workers. They can cater to the prejudices against Rome which are latent in every non-Roman heart. They can argue against "peaceful coexistence" and sound plausible. They can use the newest expressions of unity further to divide Christians. Yet men given to the ecumenical spirit will not find it possble to waver in the presence of such tactical advantages to the anti-ecumenical forces. Ours is not the first time which has been faced with an apparently insoluble ecclesiological or churchly riddle. When God first risked His Word in the world; when He set up a "divine community" and placed it in the hands of humans, He predestined all serious Christians to problems of this type.

Let this be admitted: if ecumenicity means that one can sit comfortably in the confines of the denomination of his birth and look out from there, he will see only foolishness in the movement since Rome has entered. If ecumenicity means that one in such a denomination seeks company in other groups almost like his and "irons out a few kinks of difference," then again there is no point in speaking of union or unity, of solidarity or concord. Only if one begins at the opposite pole will he be sustained. Begin with the vision of a world which is forming itself and closing itself off without Christ. Begin with the presence, in such a world, of a minority which grows smaller each day, but a minority which in its own name gives praise to His name. Move from there to the portrait of a Christianity filled with halfheartedness, theological unconcern, ethical compromise, spiritual weariness. Think, then, of only a small minority of people in the world who think, act, live, and die in such a way that non-Christians must reckon seriously with Christ's name before they "close off" and round out their lives. Now, the next move in thought is crucial. If one pictures this small minority as being confined to *his own* denomination, or to the particular kinds of churchly councils he finds congenial, he will never move further with the impulse. If he can exclude Catholicism from the cluster of those who confess the name of Christ, he is relieved of all further burden to share the ecumenical spirit. If he really believes that the spirit of Christ is not somehow formed in faithful Roman Catholics, he must act on that belief and treat Romans as he would "worldings." The Roman Catholic shares a common humanity, but no vision of the City of God. But the Protestant who so believes must prove it on his distinctively Protestant grounds, namely, the sacred Scriptures as read in the Church where sound reason is to be operative and where the heart is to be open to sound stirrings.

Does Scripture rule out any who genuinely confess the Name and profess belief in the Trinity? Does the core tradition of the Church permit the exclusion from Christian concern of those with whom one agrees basically on so many points? Does the "sound reason" so much touted by the Reformers and incorporated by the Protestants who share the Enlightenment provide a logical base for excluding Roman Catholics? What about experience, a fourth test? Can a Protestant who has shared concentration camp with a Catholic or who has been moved by the spirituality of a Catholic family turn his back on a communion he knows exists? The author's implied answers are clear. The Protestant who is led to the opposite conclusion is invited to re-examine the ways he came to it and to re-evaluate the means of decision.

What was implied in these paragraphs is *not* based on denial of the Reformation or a minimizing of difficulties that have grown up in four centuries. Viewed from the hope for perfect Christian agreement on divine revelation and the truth of the tradition let this be asserted: I do not believe that the central formal issue (the doctrine of authority) or the central material issue (the doctrine of grace) have been settled or have begun to be settled because of the new ecumenical spirit. I know of no firm prospect that they will be. It is foolish to base immediate church mission on the prospect that they will be soon. But viewed from the aspect of the world which is becoming self-enclosed apart from Christ, these fundamental differences are themselves razor thin. I am suggesting that the ecumenical spirit in the great Christians of the past half-century has been born not in the coziness of their denominations' living rooms but from breathing, elbowing contact with the world. *If and when* that is the orientation for the ecumenical spirit, *then* its fruit (in case, openness to Roman Catholic involvement) must have missionary implications.

Within Protestanism a creative minority of leadership is joining forces with great numbers of intuitive laymen to look first at the world's need and not at the Church's resources when mission is undertaken. Such a coalition is prepared to face that need with the aid of Catholic resources. Within Roman Catholicism great numbers of leaders, from the two most recent popes and through a minority of the College of Cardinals and on through the bishops and priests, have given credence to long ill-defined hopes in the laity that not only Roman Catholics but all Christians will work "with men of good will" in the face of the world's need. The formal increase of such expression has come largely in the past four years and anything written before 1959 on the ecumenical movement may be obsolete. It could not anticipate this complication to the ecumenical organization, which has come to be a simplification to the idea of ecumenical vision.

I know no way of documenting "scientifically" the missionary significance of an ecumenism which includes the Roman Catholic majority. But I invite reflection on the difference it must make to the uncommitted of the world to hear of a real brotherliness across Protestant-Orthodox-Catholic lines. No feature of the Vatican Council was more reported upon than that which revealed Roman interest in non-Roman Christians; no aspects of the papal encyclicals of recent years were more enthusiastically greeted than those which carried the broadest Christian vision. Think of the missionary significance of the prayers in the Octave for Christian unity; in a Roman Catholic Cardinal's penitent prayer at a World Council of Churches gathering; of the fact that countless theological conversations have been carried on across the line of separation four and a half centuries old. Think of the meaning of joint work in the areas of race relations and other ethical issues. Think of the missionary significance to the world when Christians re-evaluate their stands on issues of censorship, church-state relations, population growth, peace, with the whole of human need in view and the whole of Christian populace implied.

This is not to say that a concordant Church will find its battles won; the enemy will find new reasons to fight against a renewed and stronger Church. It is not to say, either, that Christians should merge energies to deceive the world that they have solved their internal problems. Division and separation are not the only unjustifiable offenses in the life of the Church, either in the eyes of God or the eyes of the world. But unities which do exist must be manifested, no matter how much this showing forth complicates the inner life of separated Christian bodies. I would rather have the burden of teaching the importance of remaining theological differences within the Church to the Church, than of teaching the world why Christians spend their energies fighting each other and trying to carry on a mission that would merely add to the number of fighters!

Coincidentally, the Pope took cognizance of both forms of the ecumenical movement within one year when in 1959-60 he both appointed a Secretariat for Promoting Christian Unity which would work on non-Roman conciliar affairs, and when he called a Vatican Council which would seek to unify the concerns of his church and open it to others. His action made John XXIII the most recognized ecumenical leader of his generation and made ecumenism a household word. Unfortunately the public response provided a kind of "cheap grace" or "free ride" for many Protestants or Catholics who think their work is done merely because there is mutual recognition. Both communions include so many half-believers and faithless; each is so far from its profession that the activities of 1959-60 should be seen to be nothing more than a declaration of independence for both communions to go about the work of re-formation. To do less would mean to see the equation of ecumenism with mere tolerance and indifferentism. Before long the headlines wear off, the novelty and curiosity disappear, and the world goes back to forming itself apart from Christ — unless the churches aggressively undertake a mission of word for and service to the world.

We have pictured Roman Catholic participation in the ecumenical movement to be necessary, inevitable, and salutary. We have acknowledged that barriers which today seem to be impassible have been erected by this participation, so far as the traditional "conciliar and organic union" tendencies in ecumenism have been concerned. How much more difficult it now is to picture "all in each place" who are baptized in Christ and who confess His name coming into a "fully committed fellowship"! But a clue for the future may be discovered in the nature of Roman Catholic participation. This is a clue which is seldom noted but which bears examining.

Enemies of ecumenism have seen in it the desire for developing a monolithic "super-Church," an overpowering power movement which would suppress local color, personal identity, and valid traditions. The exposure of Rome to ecumenism has proven that precisely the opposite spirit can be and is at work. The Secretariat for Promoting Christian Unity and the Vatican Council were trends away from papal centralism, organizational suffocation, "monolithity." The forces which *resisted* both are the forces for centralism and totalist policies — just as they often are in the anti-ecumenical groups and voices in Protestantism. The guiding spirits of Roman ecumenism have stressed what? They have stressed regionalism, the particularism of bishops, the mass in the vernacular, the retention of "local color" and the development of variety and diversity in Catholicism.

In an important essay Gregory Baum, Professor of Dogmatic Theology in Catholic seminaries in Canada and a member of the Secretariat, detailed this diversity and variety in Catholics of open tendency.[1] Baum argues not for a world Church which seeks bland uniformity and colorless subjection to papal authority. He writes of "the Church as the Family of God." He is interested in the actual, concrete historical forms the Church has taken and should take. Basing his argument on Hebrews 3:6, I Timothy 3:15, and Ephesians 2:19, he sees the Church to be a family or household. "The unity in a family is not oppressive; precisely because it is inseparable, a family permits tensions and a variety of different views. Calling the church a family therefore emphasizes that the bond of cohesion is not law but charity and that its unity is alive with Christian diversity."

His first thesis is most important. *The Catholic Church is constituted a family of apostolic churches.* Baum argues that if this is forgotten, then Catholic belief in the papal doctrine would cause Catholicism to appear to be an absolute monarchy. Rather (and even the first Vatican Council agreed), "bishops exercise their apostolic office not as delegates of the pope but as heirs of the apostles." The political parallel, he says, would be a federation "in which each province has its own authentic government though all provinces are united under the supreme authority of a central government."

> Conceiving the Catholic Church as a family of apostolic churches opens the way for a greater decentralization than she possesses at the moment, and offers a theological foundation for a greater diversity in life and piety within the unity of faith and obedience.

Baum reinforces his ideas with a quotation from Cardinal Leger of Montreal:

> The Church is not a purely charismatic society where each is free, whenever he wishes, to speak out . . . whatever comes to his mind. But neither is the Church an autocratic institution where the heads assume the sole right to speak, refusing to tolerate legitimate freedom of expression and

[1] *The Unity We Seek*, ed. William S. Morris (New York: Oxford, 1963), pp. 1ff.

debate. . . . The Church is an hierarchical community of
free men where dialogue is as much a duty as obedience.

By citing these words, so typical of those which are coming to prevail in Catholic ecumenical circles, I do not want to
obscure the gulf between Protestant and Catholic doctrines of
the Church caused by Catholic submission to one bishop
as Vicar of Christ and the Church's supreme authority on
earth. But I suggest that a situation of self-understanding
which differs from that of the past is coming to carry weight.

That the ecumenical spirit is one which seeks diversity is
also apparent in Eastern Orthodox thought. Most of the
papers in a recent Orthodox symposium reveal this.[2]

None does so more clearly than the chapter "Diversity in
Unity" by Philip Nabaa, Metropolitan of Beirut, which was
based on his lecture at the Fourth National Eucharistic Congress at Saragossa in 1961. The metropolitan stresses two
kinds of diversity: in liturgy and in regionalism. He quotes,
as shall we, Father Dalmais, O. P., on "Diversity of Rites
and Christian Unity," a reference which unfortunately forgets to remember Protestantism in its discussion of the West
but which points to the principle of variety:

> A long history, coupled with a common destiny, arrived
> at under special conditions, often difficult and sometimes
> heroic, has determined the appearance of the Eastern
> churches. The liturgy is the highest and most perfect ex-
> pression of the character, and through it of the soul, of
> these churches. One cannot isolate it or wrench it from
> its living setting. A liturgy is the sacred expression of a
> human community at the moment when Christ permits it
> to take part in the priestly action whereby he takes humanity
> with him to the Father. This humanity is not simply a
> gathering of disembodied individuals but is made up of
> human communities, gathered by a common destiny. The
> Church takes over the community concerned in order to
> transfigure it, and the community in turn is moulded by a

[2] *The Eastern Churches and Catholic Unity,* ed. Maximos IV
Sayegh (New York: Herder and Herder, 1963).

spirituality, a theology and customs all having juridical sanction. This view of what the Church's life means in concrete terms may have been somewhat lost sight of in Western Christendom, which allowed itself to be fashioned over the centuries by the Latinism of the Roman church, modified only by a variety of local temperaments and ethnic and national conditions. The historical background of the Eastern churches, inheritors and living witnesses as they are of the great cultures of the Mediterranean, has given them a deep sense of the Church's roots in the soil and in history. Diversity of rites, with all it implies, is one of the points on which they can make a unique contribution to solving the problems faced today by a Church that has outgrown the limits of its Mediterranean cradle and must show by its behaviour that it is truly catholic. That is, it must show itself capable of taking over all human cultures without favoring one against another.

The other stress is on "internal autonomy." While the East has less sense of conflict between its accustomed regard for regional patriarchs and the Roman Pontiff than do Protestants, of course, yet there is something in Orthodox insistence on regionalism which parallels many kinds of Protestant interest in diversity. Ecumenism, for the East, does not mean an impoverishment in texture but rather an enrichment; it does not mean a surrender of local color but rather an enhancement.

Near the beginning of the book we reproduced a simple-minded and clear four-way division of the Christian world:

    1. *The Catholic Church, constituted as a family of apos-*
    2. *Eastern Orthodox*
    3. *Protestants within the Ecumenical Movement*
    4. *Protestants Not in the Ecumenical Movement*

This could be revised in the light of current aspirations to read, more theologically:

    1. *The Catholic Church, constituted as a family of apos-*
       tolic churches which accepts the infallible magisterium
       of the Roman Pontiff.
    2. *The Catholic Church, constituted as a family of apos-*
       tolic churches which reject the infallible magisterium

> *of the Roman Pontiff but which accepts the magisterium of Eastern patriarchs.*
>
> 3. *The Catholic Church, constituted as a family of apostolic churches which, faithful to the Protestant principle of self-criticism, have formally met to bear united witness in the ecumenical movement.*
>
> 4. *The Catholic Church, constituted as a family of apostolic churches which have not yet formally become involved in bearing united witness.*

The definition has now been given the assignment of saying much more, and thus has lost its simplicity. But despite its cumbersome character, it preserves the simplicity of the key phrase "constituted as a family of apostolic churches." How different this definition is from the ones against which it militates! For instance, Baum is fighting off the view of "many Christians, inside the church and outside, who conceive of the Catholic Church as divided into two parts, the pope and all others, and claim that all power and teaching authority belongs to the pope while submission remains the lot of the others." Metropolitan Nabaa is staving off the critics who believe that Eastern Orthodoxy's involvements with Rome might lead to submission to the Roman Pontiff in the interest of bland uniformism or that involvement with Protestants might lead to the relaxation of historic attention to a variety of Eastern partriarchs. Protestant ecumenical leaders are warding off those who believe that both councils of churches and mergers between churches will lead to some sort of ill-defined but feared "super-church."

If Catholic churches balance their assets by the liability that they veer toward authoritarianism, Protestants balance theirs by their tendency toward anarchy. The ecumenical movement has brought together these two kinds of "families of apostolic churches" to bear witness to each other, to learn from each other, to come to show forth more unity, but not to create a formless, normless super-body. Eastern Orthodoxy in its accent on tradition has brought a sense of "ecumenicity in time" which Protestantism sometimes lacks. Roman Catholicism, by its sense of being one Catholic Church though it is constituted a family of apostolic churches, has brought a sense of "ecumenicity in space" in its diversity-in-unity. Roman Catholicism also brings one other element which may suggest forms which denominationalism and tradition might take as the ecumenical movement is transformed. I refer to its religious orders. True, these varieties are held together by common acceptance of the Roman Pontiff and assent to formally stated Catholic dogma. But there is a tremendous variety of colors, textures, and traditions of "feelings" in these orders which may provide a clue as to the future of the movement.

The clue for this is taken from a passage in the writings of Gustave Weigel where he refers to the analogies between these orders and Protestant denominations. After observing certain tendencies in the ecumenical movement Weigel comments, not without some implied criticism:

> If [these tendencies] should grow stronger in the [World] Council, the churches will tend to become like religious orders in the Catholic Church — different modalities of life and worship implying no substantial difference, so that the member of one group could worship and communicate freely and legitimately in the services of the others. A closer union of churches would develop, but at the cost of the conviction of so many churches, namely, that their creed, code, and cult are warranted by the truth of the gospel, while others are not . . . . This would dissolve sectarianism.[3]

I am not saying that the World Council of today brings churches to this point or that Weigel, from without, can really accurately pose the problem of "union now" and "truth first" as they appear to Protestants. But much can be learned formally from his expression that one day what had been

[3] *The Eucmenical Movement — A Catholic Approach* (London: Geoffrey Chapman, 1958), pp. 24f.

denominations will become "different modalities of life and worship." "Life and worship" do not exhaust the meanings of the Christian faith; they still leave the issues of "faith and order," but they also reveal the possibility of retaining diversity in one church while lessening the offense of division. What will "die" to give birth to such a new life? Some kinds of autonomy will die, some preferences for certain jurisdictions and certain kinds of clubs of people will die; some attachment to trivia will have to be left behind. Some ecclesiastical self-centeredness will have to die. Theological particularity will not disappear, but it will be placed into a new setting: the witness to truth will be undertaken in a family of apostolic churches mutually accepting each other, and not in the privacy of competitive denominations.

Jean Canu has described the process of expressing and absorbing differences within the context of unity in the Catholic orders. He observes the great disparity of claims between orders at their birth. But finally

> two ways of going to God [moved until] there was not so much conflict as rivalry, not so much rivalry as emulation and finally a reciprocal interaction, which facilitated mutual understanding and the development of a more complete and harmonious . . . life.
> The same phenomenon has appeared in every age of the Church's history and can still be seen today: Orders apparently opposed, if not contradictory, unconsciously come to model themselves on each other, until their theoretical differences seem to have a purely conventional value, and we find in one what we thought only to find in the other, and *vice-versa.*[4]

Different modalities of life and worship, having many differences which have a purely conventional value — this is what we see coming to pass among ecumenical thinkers and their denominations. This model provides little guidance

[4] *Religious Orders of Men,* tr. P. J. Hepburne-Scott (New York: Hawthorn, 1960), pp. 25f.

for those institutionally responsible for the ecumenical movement. But they are few in number. The vast majority of Christians need only some model which will give them confidence that increasing interaction between churches need not mean an impoverishment but can mean an enrichment. For the sake of the mission of the Church, it had better. The man who asks, "Why don't the churches get together?" is not asking for one formless glob of churchiness. The church which does not surprise, cause wonder, create a sense of mystery, move in a variety of directions, represent many things, will soon be dismissed as monotonous and wholly predictable.

The validity of variety was classically portrayed in a passage of Thomas Aquinas, one which is not lacking in missionary potential! He speaks of the "diversity of states and offices" just as we are speaking of "different modalities" which were once denominations. This diversity serves

> first, the integrity of the Church, second, the carrying out of the Church's action, third, the dignity and beauty of the Church. First, essential perfection, which is single and simple in God, is broken up and manifold in creatures . . . . Second, different men should be appointed to different jobs, so that the Church's work may be carried out in a more orderly and expeditious fashion . . . . Third, splendour and richness should be set out and arrayed. *When the Queen of Sheba had seen all Solomon's wisdom, and the house that he had built, and the sitting of his servants and the attendance of his ministers, there was no more spirit in her.* And again, *in a great house there are not only vessels of gold and of silver, but also of wood and clay* (*Summa Theologica*, 2a-2ae, clxxxiii.2).

In 1925 the United Church of Canada was formed, incorporating among others Methodists and Presbyterians. It is possible to walk into many churches existent before 1925 and determine whether they were Methodist or Presbyterian. This observation is sometimes used as a criticism of Canadian ecumenicity and said in derision of the United Church. Just the opposite is true. For forty years the congregation has joined in a united witness which has served to minimize the offense of division. But it has permitted what riches it has brought (and what naturally retarding factors it has brought) to be set out on the table. What is meaningful can be picked up and transformed. What is disruptive can wither and die. The diversity of "different modalities" in ecumenism guarantees that what is psychologically, sociologically, and most of all theologically valid may endure.

Roman Catholicism, by seeming to frustrate hopes for "organic union" of churches and by complicating conciliar forms of reunion, may be simplifying the missionary task in ecumenism by showing how the ecumenical spirit is not incompatible with a variety of modalities, orders, forms.

Chapter Seven

THE DEATH AND BIRTH OF DISCIPLINE OR: EVERY MAN HIS OWN ECU-MENICAL MOVEMENT

IN THE SUMMER OF 1960 THE "ELITE" OF EUROPE'S CHRIStian youth met at Lausanne, Switzerland, for an ecumenical gathering. Impatient with existing forms of church life, wearied of the negotiating that goes on in ecumenical conversation, bored by existing disciplines, the young people wanted to receive the Lord's Supper together. When cautioned against such a practice because their parent church bodies had not yet produced documents which would have placed them in detailed agreement, the youth decided to act. In effect, they commandeered a cathedral and participated in the communion in an "undisciplined" situation.

This kind of activity is unnerving to the careful planners of the ecumenical movement as it is offensive to many elders in the parent church bodies. No doubt considerable soul-searching went on during and after the event in the lives of those participants from churches which do not practice open communion. I am not using the occasion to point to a model for interrupting ecumenical tedium and ecclesiastical finesse. While fully understanding the motives of the people involved, I want to use the occasion as a parable of a certain kind of anarchy. No doubt some readers may feel that such an anarchy is implied in the argument of these pages. Can one be so impatient with the progressively more complex forms the ecumenical movement has taken in a half-century and not, in effect, come to the point where cathedrals have to be commandeered and altars taken by storm in order to jostle the movement into progressively still more complex forms?

I propose in the following pages to suggest that something quite different is occurring and must occur. Most talk of "radicalism" or "prophecy" or "judgment" in ecumenism deals with ways of shaking up the movement by dealing with idolized *churchly* forms. Instead, Christians will be drawn into more profound unities by focusing together on the *worldly* needs surrounding the church in all times and at all places — in other words, by focusing on *mission*. This means that not cathedrals but capitals must be "commandeered"; not altars but market places must be stormed; it is not in sanctuaries where ecumenical progress is to be noted so much as in the streets. "God wants to be praised in the middle of the world," and the ecumenical spirit will advance when it is moved outside the church doors. If this occurs, the disciplines of church life can be respected and retained for whatever validity remains in them.

Anarchy as a permanent way of life is not a possibility for either divided or uniting churches. "If you would see disorder, go to hell," advised Puritan divine Richard Sibbes. On second thought, said Sibbes, even in hell there is order, for there are ranks of devils. Something can be said for a disciplined "interim ethics," or way of acting "in the meantime," an ethic which respects the existing problems of denominations, confessions, and traditions. This may appear to be a counsel of conservatism, but it hides an inner radicalism that cannot be matched by the day-to-day attempt to be iconoclastic and to set one's self constantly above the mind of the Church in a kind of higher individualism.

Ecumenical anarchy directed to forms of church life can be a denial of the doctrine of the Church which is ostensibly being served by the ecumenical spirit. Rejection of all disciplines and forms of church life can amount to the creation of homemade churches alongside the real Church. It may lead to the creation of false elites, clubs, momentary organizations that will soon be institutionalized themselves. Something must be said for the institutions which grow up "naturally" and through the consensus of numbers of people. What is needed is not less conformity in an external way to institutional forms. What is needed is an inner freedom from their tyranny. Man, says Wolf-Dieter Marsch, has created a cosmos of institutional order around himself which in its turn becomes a cosmos of its own, with laws, customs, and cultural habits that govern man and limit him in his basic freedom.

> As an influence which already shapes every free action, institutions are, therefore, on the one hand, essentially necessary in order to make alienated action possible at all; on the other hand, however, they are felt to be a constant stumbling block, preventing man from freely developing his creative forces of self-realization, and confronting him with the dilemma of choosing between adaptation or a critical attitude toward existing institutions.[1]

Marsch leaves us with an apparent dilemma which I have tried to complicate by suggesting a "fusion": one must *both* adapt and retain a critical attitude. What a letdown! A reader who has stayed with the argument and heard talk of "instant ecumenicity" may have been looking for a grand plan leading to "the coming Great Church." Instead, he hears a suggestion that as new ecumenical forms evolve one must adapt to what exists and somehow sustain a critical attitude toward what exists. Can this be sustained? It cannot, if one's eye is on the institution for its own sake, if ecumenical concern remains "church-centered." Only an ecu-

[1] Wolf-Dieter Marsch, "The Concept of Institution in the Light of Continental Sociology and Theology," in Walter Muelder, *Institutionalism and Church Unity* (New York: Association Press, 1963), p. 44.

menical spirit which is daily oriented toward mission to the world will be able to sustain such a psychological burden in an impatient Christian.

If this be so, one must speak, in a sense, of "every man his own ecumenical movement." From the first page until now we have rejected those approaches to ecumenism which suggest that man is justified by belonging to denominations which have ecumenical connections. Man is not justified by his affiliations. Within these organizations he participates in disciplined forms to which he adapts and with which he remains uneasy and which he tries to change. Each day he is "his own ecumenical movement" as he picks up allies and associates for the tasks of the day. No one can serve in detail as a model for another in this task. But something like Denis de Rougemont's personally constructed dialogue must occur in each:

> I imagine that such a nonconformist curiosity in this realm may explain my fruitful friendships, whether successive or simultaneous, with men whom, in so many respects, everything seemed to set in unremitting opposition to each other: from Karl Barth to Andre Breton or Teilhard de Chardin; from the strictest theologians of Europe and the United States to the writers furthest from all dogma, although regarding themselves as Christian; finally, certain spiritual leaders of Islam and India. Lacking the power to establish an actual dialogue between these extreme figures who touch me so nearly but remain convinced that they have nothing to say to each other, I have composed my personal dialogue. . . .

> Man does not live by discipline but by assimilated truth . . . . There is no Church without orthodoxy, which is *rectified* knowledge (*recta cognitio Dei,* in Calvin's words) as it must be preached by 'ministers of the Word' and communicated by those who serve the sacraments. But in the life of the spirit, which is not collective, Spirit alone can show the way to the appropriation of truth. Yet Spirit reveals that there are as many ways as persons created by it.

> Sometimes I tell myself that these ways are all "heretical" in the eyes of the Church's coherent doctrine, but redeemed by their convergence beyond the various *anathema sit*.[2]

"A personally constructed dialogue" which involves common words and common action by persons who live in disciplined, orthodox communities can produce a clearer witness to the world than mere conformity to new ecumenical forms themselves. Many a Roman Catholic, forbidden by canon law from participating in a local community's Union Thanksgiving Service, may appear to be and may be more ecumenical than those who attend such a service and then return to the competition of denominations. He is sustained by his view of the Church's mission to the world. Using him as a model does not serve to justify ecumenical plateaus or to relax the quest for profound documents of reunion or fully shared worship. These latter will be produced by common study that grows out of common work.

I see no other way to address, in particular, the young people of the Church. Once they perceive the narrow edge of significance to the whole Christian venture; once they understand the precariousness of Christ's cause in the world; once they grasp the ecumenical spirit — shall they live in spiritual suspended animation until ecumenical forms meet their standards? On them the future of the movement depends. Very often they share the world's bored unconcern over existing forms. Some of them will soon settle down to become the "pillars" who no longer want ecumenism: they are helping to keep the organization going. But between the boredom of the outsider and the tedium of the denominational hack, a new generation can become part of the kind of "elite" the movement needs. Not all of them will be free to attend meetings like the one at Lausanne; not all will

[2] In *The Christian Opportunity,* tr. Donald Lehmkuhl (New York: Holt, Rinehart and Winston, 1963), pp. viiff.

have the experience of "commandeering" a cathedral and sharing a common Supper. But many of them are participating in *ad hoc* world-oriented ecumenical impulses (freedom rides, campus Christian movements, etc.) which permit "personally constructed dialogue." These practical expressions of ecumenism better commend the Christian cause to the world than do countless ecumenical pronouncements or tidy moves on the chessboards of ecumenical mergers and conciliar revisions.

A mature denominationalist might paraphrase the old song with its question, "How are you going to keep them down on the farm" of their own church bodies — after they have had the uniting experience which Christian work and witness brings across the lines of the church bodies? Will not such a spirit mean the death of denominations? In a sense, yes. The ecumenical movement is conscious of this "dying," as evidenced by a line from a Faith and Order document of 1960: "Achievement of unity will involve nothing less than a death and rebirth for many forms of church life as we have known them." Dying is always a terror. One does not plan to "like" it. But the Christian sees in the pattern of death and rebirth a greater boon than mere life. Achievement of unity cannot come without discomfort and death to existing forms. Whoever is responsible for those forms will be threatened; whoever has made them his security will resist change.

But is all such resistance to come only from existing forms? Will not new institutions also immediately work for their self-preservation? Many observers find the World Council of Churches to be a "domesticated revolution" already burdened by patterns of its own life and bureaus and boards. We have already cited a built-in conservatism in the charter of the World Council of Churches, in the token paid to the autonomy of existing church bodies. "Negotiations" between these bodies and within the Council will normally be an undramatic affair. The actual moves toward concord between Rome and the

East and the even more remote possibility of new under-
standings between Catholicism and Protestantism will involve some technical talk and wearying work. Few of these
technicalities will inspire Christian imaginations. During their
enactments the world will continue to "close itself off" apart
from the word of Christ if Christians only tend to their
institutions. It is the Church in mission that generates en-
thusiasm and concern.

At present there is little prospect that a large number of
seminarians, young ministers, collegians, and youthful members
of congregations will become directly involved in ecumenical
organizations. Their role will be less in the formation of
such organizations at their centers than in the re-formation of
such by the way people act and think where they themselves
live and work. Many of these, if they daily and in every
way choose to "break the rules" and violate the disciplines
and disdain the orthodoxies of their own families, will find
themselves "between communities," not at home in any em-
bodiment of the Church.

Such persons will find that their histories will be largely
bound up with Methodism or Lutheranism or the North-
eastern District or with First Baptist Church. We have been
suggesting consistently that none of these institutions in
isolation has a sufficiently deserving history to summon the
best energies of Christians. What can be done? Negatively,
to borrow Peter Berger's phrase, they can engage in "sociological Machiavellianism"[3] — which, I am afraid, is the
counsel of this chapter.

Berger facetiously describes the tactic as one in which a
person "acquires scruples and keeps on cheating." "Only he
who understands the rules of the game is in a position to
cheat." He must learn the precariousness of the forms society

[3] Peter L. Berger, *Invitation to Sociology: A Humanistic Per-
spective* (New York: Doubleday, 1963), pp. 151ff.

presents him, the accidental character (in this case) of denominational patterns. Even this understanding is liberating. Then one can begin to determine in what realms he must make a choice against these forms. He can withhold co-operation from history. While Berger's last paragraph sounds cynical, it can easily be translated into well-meant Christian action:

> Another option is what we regard as the most plausible one to result from sociological understanding, one that can combine compassion, limited commitment and a sense of the comic in man's social carnival. This will lead to a posture *vis-a-vis* society based on a perception of the latter as essentially a comedy, in which men parade up and down with their gaudy costumes, change hats and titles, hit each other with the sticks they have or the ones they can persuade their fellow actors to believe in. Such a comic perspective does not overlook the fact that nonexistent sticks can draw real blood, but it will not from this fact fall into the fallacy of mistaking the Potemkin village for the City of God. If one views society as a comedy one will not hesitate to cheat, especially if by cheating one can alleviate a little pain here or make life a little brighter there. One will refuse to take seriously the rules of the game, except insofar as these rules protect real human beings and fosters real human values. Sociological Machiavellianism is thus the very opposite of cynical opportunism. It is the way in which freedom can realize itself in social action.

Whoever has failed to see the comedy in denominational self-aggrandizement and the rituals associated with it will not understand the point of this chapter. Whoever has failed to see it in an ecumenical assembly's protocol and processions will equally misunderstand it.

If ecclesiastical forms are partly facades and social fictions, to what does one attach himself with utter seriousness? Berger speaks of "compassion" and the concerns of "real human beings" and "real human values." These concepts can be translated theologically into the central Christian concerns. Dare anyone claim a monopoly for himself in his own existing churchly forms, when such concerns are cited?

In a series of magazine articles written in 1960 I advocated something like Berger's vision. Deliberately choosing dramatic terms to emphasize a point that could be lost in subtlety otherwise, I spoke of living in denominations and being faithful to their disciplines. But meanwhile, there must be "subversion," "infiltration," "encirclement," and other tactics which work toward the ultimate death and transfiguration of these forms. These tactics were subjected to some criticism: is there not in them a denial of Christian truth and discipline and a betrayal of ethics in an open-faced advocacy of this sort? This question is legitimate among those who equate the accidents of their denominational history with the whole of the Christian tradition. To those who make a distinction, the tactic appears in a different light entirely.

Such an approach never permits one to rest content with the ecumenical replacements of competitive church life. James Baldwin, the Negro author, somewhere asks whether he should be conceived of as desiring to be integrated into a burning house. So with Christianity; at its strongest, purest, truest, most alert, most disciplined it remains such a small voice among the powers of the world that it will appear to be a "burning house." What is more, the forms of the Church will constantly be found to be dying both because of the shattering creative work of the Holy Spirit and because of the re-forming activity of Christian people.

In Paul's First Letter to the Corinthians, 7:29-31, a dual attitude to the forms of life is described. This attitude is coming more and more to be used to depict what life in the institutions of the world should look like and, to the degree that churches share this institutional character, how they should look and what attitudes their adherents must hold: "I mean, brethren, the appointed time has grown very short; from now on, let those who have wives live as though they had none, and those who mourn as though they were not mourning, and those who rejoice as though they were not rejoicing, and those who buy as though they had no goods, and those who deal with the world as though they had no dealings with it. For the form of this world is passing away." This profound theological description is a biblical parallel to the "sociological Machiavellianism" described above.

Only one who learns this duality of being involved and being detached, being engaged and disengaged, departing and returning, co-operation and withholding, can understake disciplined life in the current forms of church experience while waiting for and working toward something new. Thus one can be inspired by Roman Catholic irenicism and repulsed by the politics of the Curia; he can enjoy the Methodist impulse and resent Methodist bureaucracy; he can sing the Lutheran chorales and resist Lutheran stubbornness; he can hope for the ecumenical movement and withhold awe from some of its Genevan forms.

If he wants to be a Christian and thus by definition to be involved in corporate life in Christ, however, he must see some positive ways of being related to existing churchly forms or he must devise new ones. Does one by sitting down and reckoning plan durable new forms, or will these be merely highly individualistic emphases, clubs, "gimmicks" which soon pass away? Should he put his energy into pseudo-churches or work toward seeing new life in the Church as it is now incarnated in and limited by the forms he has inherited?

The Christian is constantly asking, as he lives within his own tradition and under his inherited disciplines: How did this tradition grow? What did or does this discipline seek to safeguard? If it is removed, what will replace it? It would be a pathetic hope to think that an ecumenical bureaucracy is *per se* better than a denominational bureaucracy; that a habit of the uniting church is automatically better than one of the divided churches. But Christian thought and Christian action undertaken by persons under various disciplines and responsible across the lines of confessional faithfulness is *per se* better than competitive activity. It is better because of the witness it brings to the theological oneness of the Church and because it commends the one Lord to the world. The offense to the world is not the multiplicity of jurisdictions and bureaucracies but rather the competivite work and conflicting witness.

The ecumenical movement will inevitably be "catholic" in its essence; that is, it seeks to be inclusive and all-embracing. What we are here suggesting is that those who have been disciplined in the church forms they have inherited, even as they "withhold co-operation" from some of their elements, will be the people ready to be "protestant" inside the movement. As the Ecumenical Church is being formed, it will also have to be re-formed. Perhaps a generation that has become impatient with the ecumenical movement can be attracted to that task.

Chapter Eight

BACK TO THE WALL; FACE
TO THE WORLD

"NO SOCIETY, ONCE IT HAS BECOME WELL-ADAPTED TO ITS environmental setting, will abandon its way of life and adopt a new one, however more . . . effective the new one may be from some objective standard, unless it is pressured into doing so by outside forces."[1]

The cultural anthropologist may talk in terms of evolutionary laws as he depicts cultural change. The historian is more open to surprise, and the Christian thinker must leave scope for the Holy Spirit to bring change. But all three can agree that ordinarily great changes among great numbers of greatly adapted people will occur only through pressures of change from without.

The setting of Christian missions in an era of interchange, transportation, and communication brought people together to face the first half-century of the ecumenical movement.

The social settings of Christian mission in an era of secularization, by which we mean that the world is completing itself and "rounding itself off" without including God's possibilities, is ushering in a second phase of ecumenical thinking.

The first phase was blessed with the initiative of students,

[1] *Evolution and Culture,* ed. Marshall D. Sahlins and Elman R. Service (Ann Arbor: University of Michigan, 1960), p. 80.

laymen, and missionaries. As this phase is coming to an end the movement is losing the attention of these groups. It would be a dreary assignment to have to go to a university campus in the Western nations and try to attract and hold an audience on the subject, "The Ecumenical Movement." Lay institutes on the subject of ecumenism are notoriously apathetic; they receive small finanical support, are poorly attended, and are participated in (if at all) with little fervor. The missionaries, so involved in the movement's destinies, are not particularly interested in its day-to-day detail. If the attempt to show forth Christian unity is to proceed further, it will have to capture the imagination of precisely such groups as these. The first group, namely students, we have used to symbolize Christians who stand between generations and between the Christian faith and secular academic possibility. Here a new world is being formed, on campuses. The second group, the laity, symbolizes the broad mass of Christian people who live most of their lives deeply involved in the world's ways; no matter how seriously they take church life, their involvement is largely tangential. The third group represents the geographical frontiers of the Church.

The ecumenical spirit will be incarnated in a movement only when and to the degree that its central concerns are handed back to these initiators of the whole tendency.

This argument does not imply that the denominational leaders, the professional theologians, the drafters of documents be removed from the scene. There are a variety of gifts, but the same Spirit. What it does mean is this: that "back-room boys" (what one Faith and Order spokesman called his movement's experts) be just that. They are to undertake the quiet and undramatic work to which they are called as an essential element in the movement. But they should not represent the facade, the public face, as they now appear to be doing.

If this line of thinking is followed, then one could say that this book has not been about "the ecumenical movement" at all. It has concerned itself with the world and with the nature of the Church in the world. Among the features of the whole life of the Church which must be reckoned with is its essentially united character. But while this "one" character is essential and central, it is not the only aspect of the Church's life which concerns the world. This book, in that sense, has concerned itself substantially with the mission of the Church in the world and accidentally with the question of unity.

What happens when the missionary precariousness of the Church is forgotten? At a recent ecumenical discussion on some churchly practices a German evangelical bishop was describing the many kinds of activities in which he engaged in a concentration camp but which he would not attempt now. When asked why certain practices were licit then but forbidden now his answer was direct. "Oh, now we are in normal times. Then the Church was *in extremis.* Then we were back to the wall. In times of emergency the Church thinks and acts in a different way than it does in normal times."

This is the "ecclesiological mentality" which is a constant threat to ecumenicity. The students, laymen, and missionaries who regard the movement at all do so with the fear that the extremely precarious situation of the churches will be forgotten by those who draft the documents, do the negotiating, make the moves on the denominational chessboards. The neglect or disdain shown the movement by such Christians in exposed positions does not represent an abandonment of the ecumenical end but only of the current means. They are aware that we are still in what W. A. Visser 't Hooft calls a "semi-ecumenical age," but they have greeted it with a para-ecumenical movement. That is, for them the movement has proceeded far enough to equip the Church for mission, and when the Church engages wholeheartedly in mission it will show forth further unity. To them the institutional forms of ecumenism may actually retard the missionary and ethical hope.

At many ecumenical seminars a student, a layman, or a misionary will raise such concerns. Often he will do so with what appears to be impatience, thoughtlessness, and bad manners. He is not listened to. He is treated courteously but regarded as if he simply is not aware of the complexities of discussing churchly reunion. Those who rejected him may be correct. He probably does not know of the complexity. What is more, he could not become interested in it even if he were invited to inform himself. He may seem obnoxious, a complicating factor. But it is about the world to which he is exposed that the Church must concern itself. Seldom is the Church given problems in the tidy forms it seeks because it has prearranged institutions to manage them. Ordinarily they come as embarrassments and in confusing ways.

When the world still asks, "Why don't the churches get together?" after they have been doing so for a half-century; when we can say, "The ecumenical movement hasn't caught on with church people," even though the vast majority of them are directly and centrally involved, then we must conclude that other concerns are on their minds to crowd out what is happening before their eyes. Sometimes these concerns are destructive of central Christian goals. Among these are local loyalties and denominational competition. Just as often they may be legitimate ones, based on Christians' views of the setting of the Church *in extremis*.

Critics of the ecumenical movement from the other, the self-defensively denominational side, have not been slow to point out that whatever of ecumenism there has been has been motivated by the world's pressures of change. Representative of these is the argument of J. Marcellus Kik in *Ecumenism and the Evangelical*.[2]

His book is a thoroughgoing critique of the ecumenical spirit as being a denial of denominational (and specifically *his* denomination's) truth. When he discusses motivations of ecumenism he comes across the following:

> *First,* the world situation presents a powerful incentive to act with Christian unity. Fearful and dreadful consequences of destructive hydrogen and atomic bombs should unite all Christian forces to work together . . . .
>
> *Second,* the conquest of the heathen world forms a powerful drive for the Christian church to become united.
>
> *Third,* a frequently mentioned incentive to ecumenism is the prevalent secularism. Education, arts, professions, economics, politics, all are being dominated by secularism . . . .
>
> *Fourth,* the growing power and influence of the Roman Catholic Church creates a motive for a united Protestant church that has great popular appeal . . . .
>
> *Fifth,* a common complaint expresses concern that divided Protestantism cannot speak with one voice and act with united purpose. An organized united church will provide an effective agency to speak to the world with one voice . . . .
>
> *Sixth,* the most powerful motive for the establishment of a world-wide church is the conviction that God desires his worshippers to be within the framework of one ecclesiastical structure . . . .

Needless to say, since Dr. Kik has an answer for the ecumenical movement (everyone should join his church and agree with Dr. Kik), he finds the existing movement at fault on all six points. For our purposes, we need only note that reasons "four" and "five" are not under discussion here, for the ecumenical spirit is no longer (if it ever legitimately was!) identified with Protestant self-aggrandizement at the expense of Roman Catholicism. But Kik's first three and

[2] Philadelphia: The Presbyterian and Reformed Publishing Company, 1958, pp. 44ff.

his sixth reason for being ecumenical state the case fairly well. The world situation leaves no room for a divided Christian presence. Missions cannot be understood "Christianly" in a divided Church. The secular world is making itself felt behind the facades of Christian institutions; finally, the Bible knows no definition of the Church divided.

From the left, then, we see the heirs of those who gave birth to the movement now growing impatient with it for failing to take "world" seriously; from the right we see those who reject the forms of ecumenicity, being disdainful of the way it approaches the problem. Significantly, both agree on what the motivations for ecumenism should be. Recessive among these concerns are church-centered ones which have come to dominate in official Orthodox, Roman Catholic, and Protestant talk. We are developing "two cultures" of ecumenical spirit; they are in danger of breaking communication with each other because their expectations and means differ so. Only a renewed sense of mission will draw the two together.

Something must be said for those who represent the bishop in Germany, those who work for establishing serene modes of life "for normal times like ours." It must be agreed that the human person cannot tolerate a situation of perpetual crisis. If one cries, "Wolf! Wolf!" at all times he will not be heard when the ultimate threat does come. One can issue announcements of the Church's crisis like publicity handouts until their very numbers cause them to lose force. Something can be said for the need of sustained and quiet ministries, durable institutions, continuity.

Any observer of human institutions and of church life soon comes to see, however, that these ministries and institutions will develop automatically and almost without attention to detail. The human needs which are expressed in protective institutions, in cuticles, in defensive walls will be met inevitably — in divided or united churches. But mission will mean a constant unsettling of these resolutions, a regular uprooting from what is comfortable and congenial. For this reason it demands and deserves emphasis constantly.

It remains, then, only to discuss this "mission" of the Church and to see it in relation to the questions of unity and truth. We have agreed that if missions means snatching a number of souls away from the world into tightly organized ecclesiastical bodies, then the competitive principle is effective. Statistically, one will be productive in missions most of all if he proselytizes, disparages other Christian endeavor, undercuts other Christian workers, believes that he alone possesses the truth, cajoles people into accepting the advertisements of his confession. While the ecumenical churches stand under judgment in comparison to the missionary zeal of the anti-ecumenical forces, they must be awakened to mission on a different basis and must resist the temptations to compete. For competition is a short-range exploitation of the Christian relation to the world.

The beginning of Christian mission in a secularized world which is not predisposed to Christianity can be summarized in the term "presence." A. M. Henry has detailed this concept: "Two major facts today urgently demand the development of a mission theology: on the one hand, there is the prodigious increase of unbelief in the world, and, on the other, the seeming lack of credit attached, in this same world, to the Word of truth which is our salvation."[3] In such a world the Church is "implanted" first by being present precisely at the most difficult locations: among the peoples who have never been exposed to the Christian word; among those who have left it behind — in factory and university and in social classes which have not found Christian forms congenial.

The Christian "presence" can achieve its mission only if it

[3] A. M. Henry, O. P., *A Mission Theology* (Notre Dame: Fides, 1962), p. 1.

represents the whole Christian Church. The man and the cell which engage in making this "presence" felt will inevitably be marked by a divisive label: Baptist, Roman Catholic, Mennonite. But a man can show in every move that he is engaging in the Christian presence and not helping his denomination to "seek its own." In this presence the Church makes its way in countless fashions: by word and work and even by silence. Out of this attitude it begins to commend Christ to the world.

The time will come when one can aggressively "present Jesus Christ." Such an approach does not violate the person or integrity of the secularized person who is the object of missions. A "failure of nerve" in the Western Church has entered missionary discussion because it is felt that all attempts to extend the reconciling circle can be accomplished only at the expense of already valid forms of religion. Who gives Christians the right to assert the superiority of their religion? But the Christian presence and the modes of communicating by presenting Jesus Christ are directly the opposite of those modes which seek to make Christianity a superior religion. Superiority is the language of imperialism; the Christian comes to the secular world as its servant.

What confidence is there, after the example of the nineteenth century, that renewed mission will not inevitably mean renewed competition and intensified division? Of course, the risk is there. But neither world nor Church appear the same after another half-century of secularization and of ecumenical conversation. The mission of which we speak is not necessarily to be oriented to competitive denominational "sending" boards so much as to the Christian presence wherever Christians are. This kind of mission is most readily engaged in by laymen, by travelers, by marchers and picketers, by quiet infiltrators of campus circles.

If this Christian presence in the world is to be felt before Christians agree on everything, what will this do to the concept of truth? The "evangelical" argues that to be involved in the ecumenical movement means to be involved in exposure to other truths with the risk that one's own particular truth will be lost, and that inevitable compromise of truth is implied in the conversation itself. The calls of "instant ecumenicity," "ecumenicity by public relations," "every man his own ecumenical movement," "withholding co-operation from history" all seem to be deliberate and perverse twists on the call to witness to and contend for truth.

Every poll we have seen, every common-sense observation we can make leads us to one conclusion: that anything Christians might try *will do more justice to truth* than the competitive system they now inhabit. The cafeteria line of denominational truths has produced a weariness which is at the base of that relativizing which itself undercuts mission. The denominational system which was designed to protect particular Christian truths has served instead to remove the question of truth from the market place of ideas. Inside the ecumenical movement and even more inside the "para-ecumenical" interruptions a more lively debate and contention goes on. Theological recovery in our time has been more marked in the ecumenical movement than around it. Alertness to the world produces both the reuniting impulse and the contention for truth.

It is wholly intolerable to picture an ecumenical solution in which one is expected to teach his child something less than and other than the truth. It is a denial of Christianity to say, "I believe," where one does not believe or to confess less than what one believes for the sake of superficial unity. True, there will be the "relative sacrifice of conscience" or "relative sacrifice of intellect" which now goes on within denominationalism. No one — let us hope and suppose — finds everything satisfactory in any institution, yet he does not "go it alone." In ecumenical forms, as we have also contended, there is something of the comedy which one must view with detachment; there, too, one withholds co-operation from history for the sake of human goals and a divine vision.

"Truth divides," Father Gustave Weigel reminds Protestant ecumenicists as he invites them to be united to Rome's claim. Yes, truth divides; but do denominational "truths" in their current form represent the full Truth that is Jesus Christ? Truth divides when that truth is the wholeness, the reality of God shown forth among men in Jesus Christ. Truth divides Christ from anti-Christ, Christian from non-Christian, believer from unbeliever. But the quest for that truth is undertaken more seriously across the lines of denominational accident, despite the separations of tradition, and through the means of distinct confessions. What we seek today are what Denis de Rougemont calls "open orthodoxies."

"Let us unite in the hope that we shall agree," says T. S. Eliot from the vantage of Anglo-Catholicism as he parodies the "pantomime horse" of ecumenism. Not at all. Let us unite insofar as we have agreed; let us unite for the sake of mission. Let us then study and talk and learn and pray in order to agree.

Once more we listen to Gustave Weigel as he speaks of the unwillingness of the World Council of Churches to define itself "ecclesiologically" (as a Church): "The refusal to make an ecclesiological commitment is really an ecclesiological stand." Precisely. The existence of ecumenical conversations, shared work, shared prayers and concerns is a commitment: those in whom the Spirit of Christ is formed have already been found to be united. They seek a fuller expression of unity. They have failed to communicate their existing unities to a world. In so doing they have failed to meet what spiritual strivings and hungers the secular world presents. They have perpetuated competitive institutions. They have failed to capture the imagination of those people in the Church who are most exposed to the world, most ready to undertake an effective mission. Such people cannot wait for the ecumenical movement to bring things to a final form. They can be impatient with what they have inherited; they can help bring about the death of existing forms as they see the rebirth of others. They can find themselves implied in a prayer "that they may all be one" *so that* the world may believe.